Resilience in Life and Faith

The Bible Reading Fellowship
15 The Chambers, Vineyard
Abingdon OX14 3FE
brf.org.uk

The Bible Reading Fellowship (BRF) is a Registered Charity (233280)

ISBN 978 0 85746 734 8
First published 2019
Reprinted 2019
10 9 8 7 6 5 4 3 2 1
All rights reserved

Acknowledgements
Unless otherwise acknowledged, scripture quotations are taken from the Holy Bible,
New International Version (Anglicised edition) copyright © 1979, 1984, 2011 by Biblica.
Used by permission of Hodder & Stoughton Publishers, a Hachette UK company. All
rights reserved. 'NIV' is a registered trademark of Biblica. UK trademark number 1448790.

Scripture quotations marked 'MSG' are taken from *The Message*, copyright © 1993, 1994,
1995, 1996, 2000, 2001, 2002 by Eugene H. Peterson. Used by permission of NavPress. All
rights reserved. Represented by Tyndale House Publishers, Inc.

Every effort has been made to trace and contact copyright owners for material used in
this resource. We apologise for any inadvertent omissions or errors, and would ask those
concerned to contact us so that full acknowledgement can be made in the future.

A catalogue record for this book is available from the British Library

Printed and bound by CPI Group (UK) Ltd, Croydon CR0 4YY.

Resilience in Life and Faith

Finding your strength in God

Tony Horsfall and Debbie Hawker

To our family members and friends,
who by their love and care help us to remain resilient.

Contents

1

Introduction

Resilience has become a buzzword that is used frequently in everyday life. We hear about it on the news, and there are many workshops and conferences on this topic. But what does it mean, and how can we become more resilient?

Many disciplines, such as physics and mathematics, refer to resilience. When referring to humans, resilience is often thought of as 'bouncing back', that is, positive adaptation after adversity. UNICEF defines resilience as 'the ability to anticipate, withstand and bounce back from external pressures and shocks'.[1] This is a useful description in some cases, but not where people do not feel like they are 'bouncing' as they wrestle with challenges, and they may not end back where they started.

Neenan and Dryden state:

> Being resilient does not restore the status quo in your life – springing back to the way it was – but, rather, what you have learned from tackling the adversity changes you for the better and helps you become more keenly aware of what is important in your life.[2]

Timmins has defined resilience as 'the ability to make the best of any situation',[3] and Barrett and Martin say resilience is 'the capacity to deal well with pressure'.[4] Carr offers a specifically Christian description of resilience:

Resilience is having strength to fulfil the call God has given us, even when it will be painful and difficult. Resilience is staying fixed on a higher purpose, motivated by love of God, our neighbour, and the world, and supported by friends. While others let us down, we are carried by the one who called us.[5]

Take your pick from any of these definitions, as each of these has a use in some situations. It is important to remember that resilience is not static, something that we have a certain amount of for life. Our resilience can be depleted, but it can also be maintained, developed and enhanced.

Our aim in this book is to illustrate ways in which you can become more resilient yourself and help the children and adults you care about to also increase their resilience. We will illustrate different components of resilience that have been identified by research. We want to acknowledge the research that others have done and so we have included notes at the end of the book highlighting the literature that has influenced our thinking.

In this book we present our model, which we refer to as the SPECS model of resilience. SPECS stands for the following domains:

- Spiritual
- Physical
- Emotional
- Cognitive and creative
- Social and systemic

The word 'specs' is short for 'spectacles'. Those of us who are very short-sighted know that without our glasses we are far from resilient. When we cannot see what is happening around us, we feel vulnerable and ineffective. We need our specs to help us see clearly and act confidently. Similarly, we need the SPECS components of resilience in order to use our full potential and to see what to do about challenging situations. These SPECS provide clarity and help us move around our world without crashing down. To build maximum resilience, we should establish the building blocks of resilience in all five of these domains.

We will discuss each of these components of resilience by first drawing on research on this area, and then providing a biblical example of some of the factors that have been identified. It can be difficult to separate out the physical, spiritual, emotional, cognitive and social aspects of life, as there is a lot of overlap, and we are integrated beings. Bible characters do not each illustrate just one of these aspects, but several. Nevertheless, we will try to highlight these different factors to gain extra insights into different facets of resilience. Each chapter ends with some questions, which can be used for group discussions or considered individually.

Oates outlines the resilience we might look for in someone (a man, in this case) going to work outside their own culture:

> He should have the stamina of an Olympic runner, the mental agility of an Einstein, the conversational skill of a professor of languages, the detachment of a judge, the tact of a diplomat, and the perseverance of an Egyptian pyramid builder... He should also have a feeling for his culture; his moral judgment should not be too rigid; he should be able to merge with the local environment with a chameleon-like ease; and he should show no signs of prejudice.[6]

Such a person sounds resilient, but this also seems like an absurd picture of excellence, and that is not what we are aiming for. Instead, as you read and think about this material, we urge you to allow space for God's grace. It is easy to see weakness in ourselves or others. We are in good company, as the Bible is full of people whom God used despite their weaknesses. We will meet some of these along the way. Sometimes the people we think are feeble turn out to be the most resilient. As the Bible tells us, 'God chose the foolish things of the world to shame the wise; God chose the weak things of the world to shame the strong' (1 Corinthians 1:27). We should never write anyone off as being weak, because God is able to give anyone the strength they need to be resilient. We can enhance our resilience and release our potential.

You might wish to assess your current resilience as you begin reading this book. If so, use the rating scale in Appendix A, which encompasses the material covered in this book. This is not a research instrument, but it may help you to identify your strengths and weaknesses when it comes to resilience. Which seem to be your weaker areas? You might find these chapters especially helpful to study.

We will discuss the areas rated in the scale throughout the book and then return to the scale in the final chapter. If you put into practice the recommendations in this book, your resilience rating may increase by the time we return to the questionnaire.

Questions

1 Which definition of resilience do you prefer, and why?

2 Think about the timeline of your life. What have been the times when you have been most resilient (coping despite adversity, or making the best of difficult situations)?

3 What helps you to be resilient and to thrive in life?

4 Who is the most resilient person you know or have heard of? What do you think makes them resilient?

5 What Bible verses can you think of about resilience?

2

Spiritual aspects of resilience

A number of the key aspects of resilience can be grouped together as 'spiritual factors'. These include a sense of meaning; a sense of calling; hope and beliefs; forgiveness; gratitude; times of sabbath, stillness and silence; being part of a community who share a similar ethos; faith; and prayer and other spiritual disciplines.

Sense of meaning

The Jewish psychiatrist Viktor Frankl was imprisoned in concentration camps during World War II. He watched some fellow inmates succumb to 'giveupitis'. Without purpose, they had no reason to live, and they gave up and died. Other inmates, however, held on to a sense of purpose even in the most inhumane conditions. Frankl refused to give up, because he held on to a desire to be reunited with his wife. He noticed that the prisoners who cared for those around them, even sharing their morsels of food, seemed to survive longest. Frankl concluded that people could find meaning and a reason to live even in a concentration camp, and that this helped them to carry on. After his release he wrote a book entitled *Man's Search for Meaning*.[7] Frankl also established logotherapy, or 'meaning therapy', which focuses on helping people find meaning in their lives, whatever their circumstances.

People may be more prepared to endure hardship and suffering if they feel that what they are doing is worthwhile. This may be one reason why some people can endure persecution, torture or even martyrdom.[8] In contrast, people who lose their sense of purpose and become disillusioned are at risk of depression, burnout and even suicide.

Being outwardly focused and helping others can provide a sense of purpose and increase resilience.[9] Being generous to others is satisfying – as the apostle Paul said, quoting Jesus, 'It is more blessed to give than to receive' (Acts 20:35).

Sense of calling

Some health professionals, teachers, carers and people who work in the emergency services or other vocational jobs say that they are doing what they were born to do. Some parents feel the same way about raising children. Church leaders, missionaries and others in ministry can cope with difficulties without giving up, if they believe that they are doing what they were 'called' to do – that is, doing what they are meant to do with their lives. Believing that we are doing what God wants us to do can help us to persevere when the going gets tough. One woman whose husband was kidnapped while they were abroad told me, 'I know we were meant to be there.' Believing that it was right to be in that place helped her to cope without feeling guilty about travelling to a dangerous place, or blaming the organisation they belonged to.

A calling is not always to a particular job or place. It may be a calling to a certain lifestyle, such as living simply, buying ethically, having a low carbon footprint or being hospitable. Or it may be a calling to social action. For example, Revd Daniel Woodhouse and Sam Walton felt a calling to protest the fact that Britain sold fighter jets to Saudi Arabia. In 2017, these peace activists were arrested and taken to court for breaking into an airbase to protest because these war planes were being used to bomb civilians in Yemen. They were later acquitted after arguing in court that they were acting for the greater good.

Having a sense of what we are called to do can also help us to say 'No' to things that we don't feel called to do, and so avoid exhaustion. Henri Nouwen put it this way:

> You are very concerned with making the right choices about your work. You have so many options that you are constantly overwhelmed by the question, 'What should I do and what should I not do?' You are asked to respond to many concrete needs. There are people to visit, people to receive, people to simply be with. There are issues that beg for attention, books it seems important to read, and works of art to be seen. But what of all this truly deserves your time?…

> Try to give your agenda to God. Keep saying, 'Your will be done, not mine.' Give every part of your heart and your time to God and let God tell you what to do, where to go, when and how to respond. God does not want you to destroy yourself. Exhaustion, burnout and depression are not signs that you are doing God's will. God is gentle and loving. God desires to give you a deep sense of safety in God's love. Once you have allowed yourself to experience that love fully, you will be better able to discern who you are being sent to in God's name.[10]

Hope and beliefs

Resilient people have a sense of hope.[11] Hope can protect against anxiety.[12] Psychological research indicates that it is helpful to have a sense of realistic optimism, although false optimism can be less helpful, as it means that we are not prepared for the hard times that inevitably come at some point.[13]

Shadrach, Meshach and Abednego were told that they would be thrown into a blazing furnace if they did not worship a gold image. They replied, 'If we are thrown into the blazing furnace, the God we serve is able to deliver us from it, and he will deliver us… But even if he does not… we will not serve your gods' (Daniel 3:17–18). This is a good example of living in hope, and also accepting the reality that everything might not work out in this life and having peace about that, trusting in the life to come.

God did not prevent Shadrach, Meshach and Abednego from being thrown into the furnace, but he was with them in the furnace. God did not stop Daniel from being thrown to lions, but he sent an angel to be with Daniel and close the mouths of the lions (Daniel 6:19–22). God did not intervene to take the Israelites out of the desert when they were wandering around for 40 years, but he was with them in the desert and provided what they needed (Deuteronomy 8:2–3).

People with faith in God can pray for help and strength during difficult times, and can remind themselves that God is with them. 'Even though I walk through the darkest valley, I will fear no evil, for you are with me; your rod and your staff, they comfort me' (Psalm 23:4). We may go through the 'darkest valley', but God will be with us. That is realistic optimism.

The 'darkest valley' may describe our darkest times. Karen Carr has paraphrased this verse as:

> Even though I will lose loved ones, have financially lean times, deal with conflicts and misunderstandings, and face health issues, I don't have to be afraid or take control because you've got this [covered]. You'll never leave or abandon me. You are in front of me, beside me, and behind me. No threat or danger is bigger than your protection of me. I can be relaxed… because you are the one at the helm.[14]

Our sense of hope is based on our beliefs. The Bible teaches the following, which provides Christians with a secure sense of hope:

- God created us, and loves us (Genesis 1:27; Psalm 139:13; John 3:16)
- We will be forgiven if we ask God for forgiveness (1 John 1:9)
- The Holy Spirit is always with us, so that we are never alone (John 14:16; Matthew 28:20)
- We can pray at any time and know that God hears us (1 John 5:14–15; Psalm 65:2)
- If we believe and trust in Jesus, we will have eternal life (John 3:16; 11:25)
- God has provided spiritual armour for the spiritual battles we face (Ephesians 6:10–18)

See Appendix B for a 'resilience creed' listing more biblical truths related to resilience.

In dark times, I find it helpful to ask myself, 'Will this matter in the light of eternity?' Hurts, disappointments, embarrassments and problems can seem overwhelming when we experience them, but we can remind ourselves that in the light of eternity they will not be important. Taking an eternal perspective is our main source of hope and help when we face the possibility of our own death. As the apostle Paul wrote, 'to me, to live is Christ and to die is gain' (Philippians 1:21).

I met a woman in El Salvador whose house flooded every day in the rainy season. Her young child would cling to her neck as she stood surrounded by water in her home. The woman's face shone as she told me, 'We are rich, because we have God.' This is a picture of resilience – trusting God despite difficult circumstances, and believing that in eternity, 'All shall be well, and all shall be well, and all manner of things shall be well', as Julian of Norwich said.

In *The Message* version of Micah 7:7–9, we read:

But me, I'm not giving up.
   I'm sticking around to see what God will do.
I'm waiting for God to make things right.
   I'm counting on God to listen to me.

Don't, enemy, crow over me.
   I'm down, but I'm not out.
I'm sitting in the dark right now,
   but God is my light.
I can take God's punishing rage.
   I deserve it – I sinned.
But it's not forever. He's on my side
   and is going to get me out of this.
He'll turn on the lights and show me his ways.
   I'll see the whole picture and how right he is.

Hope can include believing that God can work all things for good, and believing that God is still present even in the darkest circumstances. Lesley Bilinda was a nurse working for Tearfund in Rwanda when the genocide broke out in 1994. Her husband and friends were murdered, and her home destroyed. She wrote:

It was like being in the tiny pinpoint of calm at the centre of a massive whirlwind… I have been stripped in one fell swoop of so much that made up my life – my husband, my home, my job, some of my dear friends… But at the bottom of it all, God is still there. I *know* he is still in control, and that he *will* bring good out of all this… It's inexpressibly painful. But in a way, it's a mysterious and awesome privilege.[15]

Forgiveness

Lesley Bilinda went on to write a second book, which grapples with the complex subject of forgiveness.[16] Research indicates that forgiving helps us to recover physically, emotionally and mentally, when compared with holding on to resentment.[17] This is not to imply that forgiveness is easy. Forgiveness is not the same as saying that it doesn't matter. Forgiveness involves feeling the pain and acknowledging that wrong has been done, but choosing to leave justice to God (and, if necessary, the courts) rather than seeking vengeance ourselves. Forgiveness starts with a choice. It may be a lifelong process rather than a quick and easy answer. We can forgive (with God's help) without ever contacting the other party. Forgiveness sets us free from bitterness, and helps us to grow in resilience. We also need to be able to receive forgiveness from God and from others, and to learn to forgive ourselves.

Gratitude

A substantial body of research has been conducted to explore the consequences of gratitude. For example, in one study participants were randomly assigned to one of three groups and given a weekly task to do for ten weeks. One group was asked to describe five things they were grateful for that week. Another group was asked to describe five hassles they had experienced in the week. The third group was asked simply to list five events that had happened to them in the week. At the end of the ten weeks, participants in the gratitude group reported feeling better about their lives as a whole and being more optimistic about the future than the other groups. They also reported fewer symptoms of physical illness than the other groups.[18] Other research reported in the same book had similar findings, indicating that people who practise gratitude regularly tend to be happier, healthier and more optimistic than those who don't, and also tend to have better sleep, more energy and better relationships.

Barbara Fredrickson conducted research after the 11 September terrorist attacks. She found that people who reported compassion and gratitude 'had greater resilience and were less likely to suffer depression post-9/11... Gratitude and other positive emotions seemed to exert a protective effect.'[19]

Sabbath, stillness and silence

We benefit from having rhythms in life, including times to pause and rest. The fourth commandment states, 'Remember the Sabbath day by keeping it holy... On it you shall not do any work' (Exodus 20:8, 10).

This commandment comes before the ones about not committing murder or adultery. We do not make excuses with the other commandments, saying that this week is an exception, but many Christians make exceptions concerning the sabbath, saying that it has been a busy week. Rest is essential, even at the busiest times – 'even during the ploughing season and harvest you must rest' (Exodus 34:21).

In the New Testament, we read of the continuing sabbath principle: 'There remains, then, a Sabbath-rest for the people of God... Let us, therefore, make every effort to enter that rest, so that no one will perish by following their example of disobedience' (Hebrews 4:9, 11).

Tony has written more about the theology of rest in *Working from a Place of Rest*.[20] Some people need to work on Sunday; they might choose another day for their sabbath. Whichever day we choose to be our sabbath, we benefit from having a day when we do not have to be productive, and we have unrushed time to spend with God and with people we care about. Having a day when we do not shop (and therefore do not make others work) can be refreshing. In *Keeping the Sabbath Wholly*, Martha Dawn describes the immense enjoyment that can come from keeping a weekly sabbath day of celebration and relaxation.[21]

In Psalm 46:10, God tells us to 'be still, and know that I am God'. In the western world today, most people are not very good at being still or stopping. And yet there are a lot of benefits to be gained from doing this. Awareness, slowing down and meditation have all been associated with improved mental health. For example, meditation has been found to help reduce anxiety and to reduce rumination on problems, as well as boosting the immune system. Silence may help to reduce blood pressure and heart rate, and make us more calm.[22] Moreover, if we are quiet and still we may be able to hear God's gentle whisper. By observing sabbath times, we are honouring God, as we are obeying his commands and acknowledging that work and activity are not our gods. The universe can carry on without us while we rest.

Community that shares a similar ethos

Our resilience can be strengthened if we belong to a community that shares a similar ethos and that supports us. This reduces isolation and builds confidence. A church or small group can provide this fellowship and social support, including practical, emotional and prayer support. Research with over 74,000 participants has found that attending weekly church services is associated with a significantly longer lifespan than not attending church, after adjusting for other major lifestyle factors.[23]

Resilient in faith

People from any faith or no faith can practise the principles of resilience listed above, but Christians have the benefit of these being written into a Christian lifestyle. Life has meaning when we believe that God is with us. We are called to follow God's leading, whatever that might look like in our lives. We have hope of God's help in this life, and of being with God in eternity. The Bible teaches us to forgive and be forgiven (Matthew 6:12, 14), and to have an attitude of gratitude (Colossians 3:15–17). Instead of getting caught up in pressure to succeed, the Bible encourages us to have different values and learn to slow down and practise stillness and sabbath rest. We are also encouraged to have fellowship with others who share our values and who support us with prayer and encouragement.

Perhaps it is unsurprising that research has indicated that having a religious faith tends to produce positivity (or optimism), motivation and faster recovery from trauma[24] – all of which are associated with resilience.

How can we remain resilient in our faith, and not lose our faith either gradually or suddenly? This is a difficult question to answer. Having a deep knowledge of the Bible helps, as we are reminded of what we believe, and of the hope that we have. But we need more than knowledge; we also need to put our faith into practice in order to build our lives on solid rock (Matthew 7:24–25). It helps to have people around who support us in our faith journey. This might include a spiritual director or mentor, an accountability partner or a fellowship group. Some people turn their back on God when they go through difficult life events, such as a traumatic bereavement or accident. It helps if we have already thought through a theology of suffering that allows us to respond to such crises (see chapter 8), and if we can accept that we don't have all the answers as to why these things happen. Often as people progress in their faith journey, their outlook becomes less black and white. They are less sure that they have all the answers, more accepting of doubt, mystery and unknowns, and perhaps more sure about the most central aspects of faith, such as the importance of love.[25] As we mature, we may focus more on what we *do* believe, and less on what we don't believe.

Spiritual disciplines

Something else that can be beneficial is practising disciplines that help us to feel that we are connecting with God. Gary Thomas describes nine 'sacred pathways', or spiritual temperaments, which help us draw near to God:

- activism (confronting evil through social action);
- asceticism (solitude and simplicity);
- awareness of God through the senses (such as using candles or incense);
- caregiving (serving others);
- contemplation (quiet times in the presence of God);
- enthusiasm (celebration, such as singing and dancing);
- intellectualism (Bible study);
- naturalism (experiencing God in nature);
- traditionalism (ritual and symbol, such as liturgy and the Eucharist).[26]

Myra Perrine expands upon this in her book *What's Your God Language?*,[27] explaining that sometimes our preferred way of connecting with God is different from the emphasis of our church tradition. In order to have spiritual vitality for the long haul, it helps if we can find our 'God language' and make a place for it in daily life. There are benefits to be gained from exploring many of these different spiritual pathways and letting our relationship with God permeate our whole life, and not just the head, as we practise the presence of God throughout the day.

We are most likely to be able to sustain a vibrant faith if our faith infuses all that we do and is not just a Sunday supplement. Intentional faith development[28] can include regular prayer, Bible study and worship, times of retreat, and reading about the experiences and wisdom of other Christians, including those who have maintained a strong faith during difficult times. It is helpful to have times when we reflect, either with others or through our own journalling, and review honestly how we are doing spiritually, and what would help us to grow deeper in our faith. Finally, we can determine that we will choose to be faithful to God (and honest about difficulties) whatever we encounter in life – depending not on our own strength, but on the strength that comes from God. For God has said, 'My grace is sufficient for you, for my power is made perfect in weakness' (2 Corinthians 12:9).

Building resilience in children: spiritual development

We learn a bit from what we are formally taught, but we learn more from what we experience in our daily lives. If children grow up observing people turning to God for help, they are likely to learn to do this too. If they live in an environment where people express gratitude and offer forgiveness, they are more likely to do the same. Children who hear people speaking with hope about the future, and especially about eternal life, can pick up this atmosphere of hope even in difficult times. Families can get into a habit of praying and reading the Bible together before a child even understands language, and the child will gradually learn of God's ways.

In the next chapter we will consider the life of Nehemiah, an example of someone who had a sense of calling (or a burden from God) and who lived a life of prayer and faithfulness, relying on God's strength.

Questions

1 How is your spiritual resilience at the moment?

2 What step could you take this month to increase your spiritual resilience? Will you do it?

3 What are you grateful for this week?

4 Do you take a sabbath day each week? How do you spend it?

5 How are you helping others (children or adults) to prepare for spiritual challenges?

6 In *The Message*, Psalm 27:14 states, 'Stay with God! Take heart. Don't quit.' Do you ever feel like giving up your faith? What, if anything, helps you continue in the Christian faith?

3

Resilience in the life of Nehemiah

I have a great love for the Bible, especially the stories of men and women who lived their lives by faith. Not only did they display great trust in God, but also great resilience, often keeping going in the face of much adversity. I am so glad that God has written many of his best lessons for us in the lives of his people. They provide examples for us today and inspire us to greater things.

Nehemiah is such a person. His great achievement was to take a bunch of dispirited and downhearted individuals and, in spite of much opposition and danger, motivate them to work together in a hostile environment to rebuild the walls of Jerusalem. This enormous task they achieved against the odds, and in a surprisingly short time – it took them only 52 days (Nehemiah 6:15)! Nehemiah demonstrates the capacity to deal with pressure, and to make the best of any situation. He faced so many setbacks, yet never gave up. He has much to teach us about resilience, and in particular the spiritual dimension behind this important characteristic. His story is told for us in the book that bears his name which is really his memoir. Our focus will be on chapters 1—6.

Trusted servant

Nehemiah was one of the Jews in exile in Babylon who had taken the advice of the prophet Jeremiah to settle down and wait for the day when God would lead them back to the promised land (Jeremiah 29:5–7). He lived in the city of Susa and, being a man of good reputation and sound character, had found favour with the Babylonian ruler, King Artaxerxes. He was appointed to serve in the palace as cupbearer to the king, a position of great trust and not a little danger – it was his job to taste any wine the king was to drink to make sure it was not poisoned. Nehemiah was well enculturated in Babylon, yet never lost his faith, and, while he lived in Susa, his home and his heart were still in Jerusalem.

In 458BC, the first group of Jewish exiles returned to Jerusalem under the leadership of Ezra, a priest and scribe. After much difficulty they succeeded in rebuilding the temple, but then the restoration of the city came to a halt. Some years later, Nehemiah received disappointing news from his brother who had recently returned from Judah:

> Those who survived the exile and are back in the province are in great trouble and disgrace. The wall of Jerusalem is broken down, and its gates have been burned with fire.
> NEHEMIAH 1:3

In other words, the city was unprotected and in great danger.

This news brought Nehemiah to his knees, quite literally. Sadness overwhelmed him, and he wept bitterly at the plight of the city. This was no superficial response – he continued to mourn this devastating state of affairs, fasting at the same time as a mark of his sincerity, and turning his concern into prayer. Here we see the first source of his resilience: he took his burden to God in prayer. How easy it is to become trapped in a downward spiral of despair. Nehemiah felt sadness, but he did not allow his sadness to overwhelm or imprison him. He chose to respond to the situation through the lens of his faith.

A burden from God

Nehemiah records for us the prayer that formed in his heart, and it reveals the depth of his faith and his understanding of the covenantal purposes of God (1:5–11). It also shows that, as he spent time before God, a plan developed in his mind. First, he confessed his own sin and that of the people of Israel (vv. 6–7). Then, he reminded God of his promise to restore his people to the promised land (vv. 8–9). Finally, he asked God to grant him success as he put his plan into action (vv. 10–11).

What happened to Nehemiah as he was praying? He had received a burden from God that he was the one to do something about the situation in Jerusalem. He was in fact to be the answer to his own prayers. This was the origin of his call, and, as we have seen already, people with a sense of calling tend to be more resilient. They instinctively feel that what they are doing is worthwhile, and they find a new meaning and purpose for their lives. This helps them to stick at even the most difficult of tasks.

This calling from God would require a career change for Nehemiah, and that is why he prayed that God would grant him favour before the king. He was not a free man, able to do whatever he wanted. Furthermore, he was not even allowed to speak to the king, but had to wait to be spoken to. One day, noticing Nehemiah was uncharacteristically sad, the king asked what was troubling him, and opportunity was given for him to tell his story. Boldly, Nehemiah shared his burden, and asked not just for leave but for letters of safe passage and for the timber with which to do the job. Miraculously, the king granted his request (2:1–9). From this moment on, Nehemiah was in no doubt that the gracious hand of God was upon him. The God who had called him would supply all he needed and help him to accomplish his God-given task. This wonderful answer to prayer was confirmation of his calling and would form the bedrock for his confidence as he moved forward.

The work begins

Arriving in Jerusalem, Nehemiah's first task was to survey the scene and assess what needed to be done, then to bring people together and inspire them for the work of rebuilding. His assessment of the situation was realistic – 'You see the trouble we are in' (2:17) – but his positive testimony was a great motivation to action – 'I also told them about the gracious hand of my God on me and what the king had said to me' (2:18). His faith encouraged the people to begin the work. They felt a sense of hope again.

Not everyone was happy with Nehemiah's arrival and his plans to rebuild the city wall. From the start there was opposition from a small but influential group of men who did not want to see the rebuilding of Jerusalem prosper: Sanballat the Horonite, Tobiah the Ammonite and Gershom the Arab. They were disturbed by what was happening and began to ridicule the idea (2:10, 19; 4:1–3). Clearly Nehemiah would not have an easy ride. This resistance began slowly but gathered momentum and became increasingly fierce as the project got underway. Resilient people are not surprised by difficulty and resistance. They know that nothing worthwhile is achieved without a fight. Struggle serves to strengthen their resolve.

On the ropes

With great skill, Nehemiah organised his workforce so that different families were responsible for rebuilding different sections of the wall (3:1–32). The work went well because the people were motivated to do it. Soon the wall had reached half its height (4:6). This was the signal for a concerted and sustained effort from the enemies of Israel to stop the work by fair means or foul. First, they intimidated the workers (4:7–8, 11). Then they turned their attention to Nehemiah himself, scheming to harm him physically (6:1–4), to slander and discredit him (6:5–9) and then to make him compromise (6:10–13).

The narrative reads like a boxing match, with Nehemiah on the ropes, and blow upon blow being landed on him by his ferocious opponent, and yet he remained standing. More than that, he and the people found the strength to persevere with their task, and against all odds the wall was completed, deflating their enemies and bringing much glory to God:

> So the wall was completed on the twenty-fifth of Elul, in fifty-two days. When all our enemies heard about this, all the surrounding nations were afraid and lost their self-confidence, because they realised that this work had been done with the help of our God.
>
> NEHEMIAH 6:15–16

Faith in God

At the heart of Nehemiah's resilience was his faith in God. Even secular writers recognise the part that faith plays in building resilience. Nehemiah believed that the God of heaven was in control and his purposes were being worked out (1:5). Since God had called him to this task, he would make sure he could complete it. God would be with them and grant them success (2:20; 4:14, 20). This kind of positive thinking is helpful when facing challenging circumstances. Nehemiah maintained a confident, hope-filled attitude even when things were against him. Clarke and Nicholson note that 'optimism is a clear marker of resilience'.[29] Not only did this buoyant attitude keep Nehemiah going, it also motivated the people to persevere when at times they may have despaired and given up.

Inner life of prayer

Nehemiah had a deep, inner life with God that was expressed in prayer. Instinctively, he turned to God at every moment of fear, anxiety and need. Often his prayers were short and to the point (sometimes described as 'arrow prayers'), but they reflect a dependency on God as the source of his help (2:4; 4:4–5, 9; 5:19; 6:14). At one moment of threat and danger he wrote, 'But I prayed, "Now strengthen my hands"' (6:9). Nehemiah persevered not because of his dogged determination, but because he was in touch with a source of strength outside himself. This belief in a 'higher power' is recognised as being a significant factor in resilience.

A worthwhile task

There is no doubt that Nehemiah's sense of calling contributed to the value he placed on his task. He variously described it as 'the work' (2:16), 'this good work' (2:18) and even 'a great project' (6:3). This feeling that what we do matters and that our contribution is important helps us to keep going when things are tough. It was the awareness that he was engaged in a 'great project' that prevented Nehemiah from leaving his post when he came under persistent pressure from his enemies to quit: 'Why should the work stop while I leave it and go down to you?' he declared (6:3).

Leadership skills

Nehemiah was a capable leader, with great organisational skills and the ability to motivate others towards the fulfilment of a vision. He was able to plan what needed to be done (2:11–16), inspire people to work hard at the task (2:17–18; 4:14, 19–20) and organise them towards fulfilling their common goal (3:1–32; 4:13, 16–22). When there was the danger of disunity due to a falling out among the returnees, he acted swiftly and decisively to resolve the matter (5:1–13).

Two characteristics stand out here. First, he had the cognitive ability to problem-solve, finding creative ways to respond to every attempt by their enemies to disrupt the work. Second, he remained flexible in his thinking and was able to adapt his plans to face new challenges as the situation on the wall changed from day to day. According to Clarke and Nicholson, 'resilient people are flexible in their approach to people, problems and environment'.[30] This is exactly the kind of leadership that Nehemiah displayed.

Personal integrity

Having a strong faith in God usually provides people with a clear moral compass and a desire for personal integrity, two characteristics of leaders who stay the distance. Some, sadly, do not have such a good foundation in their lives and although they may begin well, are highly gifted and appear successful, eventually they come crashing down. Nehemiah identified himself several times as being God's servant (1:6, 11; 2:20), which means he sought to live his life in obedience to God. As a result, when the dispute arose among the returnees about exploitation and injustice, he could deal with the matter because he himself had done no wrong. Unlike other governors, he had neither misused his power nor abused his position for personal gain. He could say truthfully, 'Their assistants also lorded it over the people. But out of reverence for God I did not act like that' (5:15). Likewise, when tempted to flee for his life because of the death threats he had received, he chose to stand his ground: 'But I said, "Should a man like me run away?"' (6:11).

Courage under fire

One thing that stands out in the story of Nehemiah is his exceptional courage. The hostility from Sanballat and his friends increased as the work progressed and moved from a general opposition to the work to a vindictive and intimidating personal attack on Nehemiah.

They sought his downfall and destruction through lies and threats, with slanderous letters and false prophecies (6:1–14). Leadership is a lonely calling, and when there is constant pressure to compromise it is easy to capitulate. Courage is needed.

Courage does not mean the absence of fear, but the strength to do the right thing even though you are afraid. We are reminded here that in spiritual ministry we find ourselves drawn inevitably into spiritual warfare, for behind all human opposition stands the power of the devil. Jim Packer comments:

> The real theme of Nehemiah 4—6 is spiritual warfare, and Nehemiah's real opponent, lurking behind the human opponents, critics, and grumblers who occupied his attention directly, was Satan, whose name means 'adversary' and who operates as the permanent enemy of God, God's people, God's work and God's praise.[31]

In such a context we must find our strength in God and in his mighty power, and ensure that we are daily wearing the full armour of God that God has provided for us (Ephesians 6:13–18). Only those who are inwardly fortified in this way are able to stay the distance in the ups and downs of Christian ministry.

Nehemiah's resilience is shown in his perseverance, that having been given a task by God he saw it through to the end. There is no doubt that he was in many ways an exceptional person with a unique calling, and we must be wary of comparing ourselves directly with him. Although some of us are called to frontline ministry, and to achieve significant things for God, most of us will need to show our resilience in the ups and downs of much more ordinary callings. Yet the same principle applies: the spiritual life is the basis for a resilient outer life, and we too must make sure we are deeply grounded in God. Only by being firmly anchored in God will we be able to withstand the storms of life and the trials that are common to us all.

Questions

1 Nehemiah felt a burden (or calling) to rebuild the walls of Jerusalem. Have you ever felt a burden or calling to do something (such as befriending someone, praying about an issue or a nation, telling someone about Jesus, fostering a child or joining some social action)? If not, why not consider asking God to give you a specific burden?

2 Have you ever faced opposition, ridicule or hostility like Nehemiah did? What helped you persevere?

3 Why do you think Clarke and Nicholson say that optimism is a clear marker of resilience? How are the two things connected?

4 Why is personal integrity a key component in resilience?

5 Which components of the armour of God are most helpful to you in overcoming the devil's attacks? See Ephesians 6:13–18.

4

Physical aspects of resilience

In this chapter we will consider some of the physical ways in which we can build resilience. When thinking about physical resilience, we look at factors that are likely to lead to a longer, healthier life. In a disaster, such as an earthquake, a fire or a terrorist attack, physically resilient people have the strength and energy to survive for longer, and can sometimes help themselves and others to escape. In general, it is harder to be resilient when we feel ill, in pain, weak, tired, hungry or short of breath. Thus, physical aspects are part of the picture of resilience. However, as you read this chapter please also remember that some people are amazingly spiritually and psychologically resilient despite physical difficulties such as illness or disabilities.

Regular exercise

Physical activity builds fitness, energy and stamina, and so contributes to resilience.[32] Regular exercise can improve cardiovascular health and boost the immune system. It is associated with reduced risk for many illnesses, including heart disease, stroke, type II diabetes and cancer. Physical exercise is also associated with mental health benefits.[33] Exercise can release tension and reduce stress levels and anxiety. Exercise releases endorphins, which are like natural drugs in the brain. That is why many people feel better after exercising. Doctors prescribe exercise as a treatment for mild depression.

For those of us who do not enjoy working out in a gym or pounding the streets in long runs, the good news is that even moderate exercise, such as walking, is beneficial for both physical and mental health. In the table on the next page, select the level of activity that best describes your current lifestyle, and consider whether you are willing to try the goals listed (based on the National Health Service activity guidelines for adults).[34] Be realistic in your goals, accepting that our ability to exercise tends to reduce as we grow older or if we have existing health or mobility problems.

Exercise that requires concentration can be particularly good for mental health, as you focus on the present moment and can't ruminate about problems when you are concentrating hard. Something like bouldering (rock climbing without any equipment), challenging dancing or a fast-action sport, such as squash, may be especially helpful. But any exercise can release endorphins and improve mood.

Look for ways in which you can make exercise fun. Perhaps you would like to try trampolining, line dancing, a team sport, an aerobics class or even 'welly wanging', a sport that involves throwing Wellington boots. You may have your own favourite form of exercise. Personally, I have set myself the challenge of trying to dance every time I hear music. This can include making my fingers dance while in the car, or swaying gently in church. It makes me smile and seems to boost mood – not only mine, but that of anyone laughing while they watch me!

People living in restrictive environments need to be creative about their exercise opportunities. I encounter women who serve in Islamic environments who cannot exercise in public. Some have exercise bicycles in the home or use a skipping rope or aerobics DVDs indoors. Others use tins of food for weight-training exercises.

Veteran missionary Marjory Foyle is a great role model. Even when she was in her early 90s she walked the London marathon every year, in addition to her normal daily walks. Exercise is a gift, which is good for us. Physical exercise is good, as Paul wrote in 1 Timothy 4:8, before adding that spiritual exercise is even better. There is a place for both.

Current level	Goal
Sedentary	Spend less time sitting or lying down during waking hours. Stand up and take a stretch break every 30 minutes. Intentionally move around. Leave your vehicle further from your destination so that you walk further.
Low activity	Increase the number of steps you take on an average day, keeping track of these with a pedometer. Use stairs instead of lifts, and walk up escalators.
Moderate activity	Have a brisk walk for at least ten minutes each day. Then try to build up to 150 minutes of moderate exercise a week (e.g. half an hour of exercise, five days a week). This could be walking, cycling or swimming. Alternatively, aim for 75 minutes of vigorous activity a week (e.g. jogging, aerobics, skipping with a rope or playing singles tennis). If you find it hard to stay motivated, exercise with a friend.
High activity	If you already achieve the above goals – well done. Keep it up! Aim for activity that makes you breathe faster and feel warmer, as this aerobic activity is good for your health and fitness. Try to add some strength-building exercises at least two days a week, such as sit-ups, press-ups, heavy gardening or lifting small weights. Take care you don't overdo the exercise. Don't let it become an addiction. Try to avoid physical damage from over-exercise.

Sufficient sleep

Sleep deprivation is associated with increased risk of hypertension (high blood pressure), coronary heart disease and diabetes.[35] Unsurprisingly, sleep deprivation is associated with decreased resilience.[36] Barrett and Martin state:

> The evidence suggests… that deficits in cognitive performance are likely to start becoming significant for most healthy adults if they repeatedly get less than about 7 hours of reasonable quality sleep a night over an extended period… Sleep deprivation makes us accident-prone for several reasons. In addition to affecting cognitive ability, it impairs motor function and lowers mood.[37]

When we feel exhausted, we make more mistakes, are less effective at assessing risk and find it harder to stay calm, think clearly and make good decisions. Different people need different amounts of sleep, but we can all benefit from ensuring that we get enough sleep so that we can get through the day without feeling tired or sleepy.

Often all that is needed is allowing enough time for sleep, and making it a priority. Occasionally missing some sleep to finish a project might not be a problem, but regularly having inadequate sleep can leave us feeling irritable and low, and make us less effective. Psalm 127:2 says, 'In vain you rise early and stay up late, toiling for food to eat.' It is a good habit to aim for enough sleep, so that we wake feeling refreshed. Going to bed and getting up at roughly the same time each day, whenever possible, can help establish a good sleeping routine.

If the sleeping problem is caused by light or discomfort, practical solutions may be enough to fix it (e.g. black-out blinds or a new mattress). If the problem is noise, playing white noise or using a fan to block out the noise may help. For those who find it hard to get to sleep, or who wake in the night and cannot get back to sleep, it is worth trying 'sleep hygiene' strategies. An internet search for 'sleep hygiene' can provide helpful advice. The following are some tips for good sleep:

- Avoid caffeine after early afternoon, including coffee, tea, chocolate and caffeinated drinks (as caffeine is a stimulant).
- Avoid looking at screens, such as a TV, computer or phone, for the hour before going to bed.
- Have a wind-down routine before going to bed. This might include a relaxing bath, reading a novel or some peaceful worship music and praying for rest.
- If you cannot sleep because your brain is too active, try a mental activity, such as counting down from 5,000 in threes. Do this while lying in bed with your eyes closed. Activities that are mentally tiring, dull and distract you from other thoughts should help you sleep.
- Try to concentrate on slow breathing to relax yourself. Breathe in through your nose for four seconds, hold your breath for seven seconds, then exhale through your mouth for eight seconds. Repeat this until you fall asleep.
- Do not check the time if you wake in the night, as that is likely to wake you up more fully.
- Do some exercise during the day, as this is associated with better sleep at night.
- Share any worries with someone or write them down, so that they don't keep going round and round in your head. Keep a pen and paper beside your bed so that you can write down anything you want to remember, without getting up.
- Some people find that the smell of lavender aids sleep. Others find that consuming certain food or drink (such as bananas, kiwi fruit, camomile tea or warm milk) in the evening is helpful.[38]

If your insomnia is caused by anxiety, depression or other mental health problems, we recommend that you seek help from a doctor, a counsellor or another mental health professional. A doctor might recommend sleeping tablets for a few nights in a crisis, but it is important not to become dependent on any medication that could be addictive, so health professionals will also consider what is needed in the longer term. Counsellors and other health professionals can help to treat anxiety, depression or other problems that might be causing insomnia.

If the sleep deprivation is caused by a child who wakes in the night, the passage of time and asking others to take turns with night duty (or to look after the child while you catch up with sleep in the daytime) may be the best solution.

Rest and margin

In addition to our need for sleep, we also need rest breaks during our active hours. In chapter 2, we mentioned the theology of sabbath. Here we are thinking about rest more widely.

The importance of rest is recognised in law, as daily and weekly rest breaks are a legal requirement in the workplace. In the UK, workers have the right to one uninterrupted 20-minute rest break during a six-hour working day. Workers also have the right to eleven hours of rest between working days. For example, if they finish work at 8.00 pm, they should not resume work until 7.00 am the next day. In addition, workers have the right to either an uninterrupted 24 hours without any work each week, or an uninterrupted 48 hours without any work every fortnight.[39]

We benefit from breaks during the day, a day off each week and longer holidays. Just as athletes need a rest day to allow the body time to recuperate and to reduce the risk of injury, so we all need times of rest to restore our physical and mental well-being.

Life sometimes throws unexpected challenges at us. For people who constantly function at full capacity, there is no energy left to deal with the unexpected. Difficulties can become the last straw, leaving over-extended people at breaking point. People who allow margin in their lives, including time, physical energy and emotional energy, on the other hand, are able to rise to the challenge. Thus, people who allow margin are generally more resilient when unforeseen needs arise.

Some Christians feel guilty about taking time off and holidays when there are great needs around them or when their friends cannot afford the luxury of a holiday. Such guilt may need to be addressed. Taking rest makes us unavailable in the short term, but more effective and resilient in the longer term.

As well as having psychological and physical benefits, rest is also a biblical principle (and margin also seems to be a biblical principle – see Leviticus 23:22). Isaiah 28 states:

> God will speak to this people,
> to whom he said,
> 'This is the resting-place, let the weary rest';
> and, 'This is the place of repose' –
> but they would not listen.
> ISAIAH 28:11–12

Those who refuse to rest are seen as disobedient, choosing to live a cursed life of 'do this, do that, a rule for this, a rule for that; a little here, a little there – so that as they go they will fall backwards; they will be injured and snared and captured' (v. 13).

There is always more that we could do. The world is full of needs. But even Jesus did not try to meet all the needs. He was willing to say 'No,' and we should be too. Jesus only healed one person at the pool of Bethesda, although there were many disabled people there (John 5:2–9). Jesus knew what his Father had called him to do, and he focused on that and not on everything else (Luke 4:42–44). Even when people were looking for Jesus, he made time to go away by himself, rest and pray (Mark 1:35–38). He slept in a boat while his disciples did all the work of sailing, until they woke him because they were terrified of a storm (Luke 8:23–24). He rested by a well while his disciples went off to buy food, all twelve men going to shop for the meal (John 4:6–8). Jesus knew the importance of rest, and he taught his disciples to rest (Mark 6:31). He also tells us to rest:

> Come to me, all you who are weary and burdened, and I will give you rest. Take my yoke upon you and learn from me… and you will find rest for your souls.
> MATTHEW 11:28–29

When we feel heavy-burdened and unable to rest, we might be carrying something that we are not meant to be carrying. It might be time to put our burden down and to rest.

Eating

The apostle Paul wrote that he had learned the secret of being content whether well-fed or hungry (Philippians 4:12). That is a good situation to be in. Most of us tend to be physically best able to cope with life when we are neither hungry (which can leave us feeling irritable, weak or preoccupied with thinking about food) nor overly full (and sleepy, sluggish or uncomfortably aware of what we have eaten).

Part of Debbie's story

As a child I wanted to be a missionary. But I felt that I did not deserve to eat more than was essential for life, and I lost a lot of weight. By the age of 17, I was 5 ft 4 in (1.64 m) tall and weighed only about 5 st (32 kg). I was frail and started to fall over on the street. I wanted to help starving people in Africa, but it gradually became obvious that I was starving myself. I was of no use to people in Africa until I recovered and was healthy again myself.

Fasting for spiritual reasons, to connect with God, can be beneficial spiritually. Intermittent fasting may also bring health benefits.[40] However, persistent under-eating, leading to excessive weight loss, can cause us to become so physically weak and preoccupied with thoughts about food that we are less able to help people around us.

The occasional feast can be enjoyed with gratitude, but regular overeating can lead to weight gain and physical difficulties. Being significantly underweight or overweight increases our risk of health problems. Maintaining a healthy weight and eating a balanced diet (with plenty of fruit and vegetables and a balance of other food groups) enhance our physical resilience.[41] At times of stress, it is especially important to eat well, taking in enough energy, vitamins and minerals to help us cope.

To check whether your weight is in the healthy range, see **nhs.uk/ Tools/Pages/Healthyweightcalculator.aspx**.

Drinking

The UK recommendation for health is that there is no safe level of alcohol consumption. Both men and women are advised not to regularly drink more than 14 units of alcohol a week, which would be the equivalent of about seven standard (175 ml) glasses of red wine or six pints of average-strength beer. Binge-drinking is advised against, and regular drinkers are advised to spread their drinking evenly over three or more days and to have several alcohol-free days each week.[42]

As well as carrying health risks, heavy drinking can reduce reaction times, impair decision-making, reduce the quantity and quality of sleep, lower mood, cause interpersonal problems and lead to weight gain. To enhance resilience, keep alcohol consumption within the recommended guidelines. Drinking plenty of water instead can help improve health.[43]

Smoking, caffeine and other substances

The nicotine and other chemicals in tobacco can lead to cancer, bronchitis, diabetes and heart problems. Nicotine also often causes sleeping problems. To increase resilience, it is best not to smoke.

Drinking too much caffeine (e.g. more than seven cups of instant coffee or five single espressos daily) can also be unhealthy, as it can lead to insomnia, headaches, nervousness, irritability and restlessness, all of which make it harder to relax.

Be careful with any self-medication or drug misuse, which can lead to health problems and addiction.[44]

Health checks

Following the above recommendations can help us keep physically healthy, and thus best able to cope with the demands of life. Reduce your health risks by attending any recommended health checks or screenings and following recommendations concerning medication, treatments and healthy behaviour. Keeping up with dental checks and visits to the opticians (if needed) also helps us remain on top form. Because the body is a temple of the Holy Spirit (1 Corinthians 6:19), we should do our best to look after our health. That will make us more physically resilient.

Building resilience in children: physical health

The best way to teach children is by being a good role model for them. If we eat healthily and exercise regularly, the children we care for may do the same. We can also talk to them about why we do such things. However, it is important that we give a balanced message. Children are impressionable, and they can develop eating disorders if we create over-concern about food. We should teach children that there are no 'bad' foods, and that getting a healthy balance is important.

We should also help them to switch off electronic devices before bedtime and ensure that they get enough sleep. We can teach them about the problems caused by smoking and help them to say 'No' if offered cigarettes, drugs or alcohol. Sex education is also important as they get older.

Linking back to spiritual factors: going outside and appreciating creation helps us physically

Research indicates that experiencing nature has physical health benefits, such as reducing blood pressure.[45] Experiencing nature is also associated with increased happiness and mental well-being.[46] For example, in one study people who took part in a project involving 30 days of engaging with nature were found to have sustained improvements in happiness and health afterwards.[47]

A form of therapy that is becoming more popular is 'ecotherapy', which aims to improve mental and physical well-being through outdoor activities in nature. In its broadest sense, the activities can range from gardening to spending time with animals. Exercising outdoors is also included, from walking, jogging or cycling to rafting, rock climbing or caving.

God has created a world that contains much beauty. Mountains and rivers; birds and butterflies; sunsets and stars – there is a lot to feast our eyes on, as well as much to hear, smell, taste and touch. God can teach us through nature. For example, Jesus taught us to stop and consider how lilies grow. God clothes them, so why should we worry about our clothes (Matthew 6:28–30)? And Jesus taught us that God even notices sparrows, so he certainly notices us and we don't need to be afraid (Matthew 10:29–31). God reveals himself through creation, as described in Romans 1:20:

For since the creation of the world God's invisible qualities – his eternal power and divine nature – have been clearly seen, being understood from what has been made, so that people are without excuse.

Many Christians find that when they spend time appreciating creation, they also appreciate and feel closer to the creator. God can use nature to speak to us and provide for us.

It can be helpful to take time to remind ourselves that beauty still exists in the world, especially when we encounter suffering. We might be able to do this by going outside – perhaps resting under a tree or beside flowing water, or enjoying mountain views.

General Robbie Risner spent seven years as a prisoner of war. He could not go outside, but he still managed to appreciate nature. To help him cope he developed a habit of getting up about five o'clock in the morning and beginning the day by looking through a vent below the floor of his cell, watching insects crawling up blades of grass.[48] Appreciating the beauty around us, however limited, can help us to keep going and not to give up.

Genetic and biological factors

As this chapter is about physical matters, it is appropriate to note that there are some genetic and biological aspects of resilience. Barrett and Martin report:

Studies of pairs of identical and non-identical twins have found that mental toughness has a relatively high heritability, with around half of the variation between individuals in mental toughness attributable to genetic differences.[49]

There may be little we can do about these genetic and biological aspects, but there is a lot we can do about the other half of the variation between individuals, as discussed throughout this book. In the following chapter we will consider what we can learn from Elijah about things that we *can* do to help build our resilience.

Questions

1 What exercise do you do, and is there anything you would think of doing to improve your exercise level?

2 What do you find helpful for sleep?

3 How much margin do you build into your week?

4 What one step could you take that would most improve your health?

5 How can you help others to remain healthy, including children?

5

Resilience in the life of Elijah

In 1 Kings 19 we encounter the prophet Elijah at a time of stress. He had just had a great spiritual victory on Mount Carmel, where he had challenged the prophets of the false god Baal to a contest to see who could get their god to send fire from heaven to burn up a sacrifice. Elijah won. God answered his prayers, showing up Baal as a false god who could do nothing.

We might have expected Elijah to be on a spiritual 'high' after this success. Instead, he was exhausted. This is understandable. He had climbed up a mountain, built an altar, chopped up a bull, prayed fervently, watched fire come from heaven, seen the prophets of Baal get slaughtered and run in front of a chariot all the way to Jezreel. What a day!

Then Queen Jezebel sent a death threat, saying that Elijah would be killed. Suddenly this great man of God, who had so much courage and faith the day before, was terrified. The day before, he had been confident that God would answer his prayer for fire. But when he received the threat, he was afraid and ran for his life. He ran about 80 miles to Beersheba, then beyond Beersheba to the wilderness, where he sat alone under a broom tree. 'I have had enough, Lord,' he said. 'Take my life' (v. 4). Scared by the threat of death, he asked God to let him die!

Elijah was a great prophet, but he was also human like us, and he had times when he was afraid. If he could crumble and lose faith after a great victory, then so can we. We are sometimes most vulnerable just after spiritual victories or high points. Sometimes we keep going while we are working on important projects, but as soon as we take a break from them, or go back home, we become ill or feel depressed. I find it encouraging to know that even spiritual heroes like Elijah can get stressed.

We will now consider how God helped Elijah to become more resilient at this time of stress.

Rest and retreat, in nature

Relief workers with non-governmental organisations often talk about the importance of rest and relaxation, or 'R and R'. By this they mean getting away from a stressful (and often insecure) environment and the pressures of a busy life, and taking a break away from it all. They might seek somewhere beautiful, in contrast with perhaps the bleak place where they are based. Or they might seek somewhere peaceful, away from the noise and rush of daily life. Some retreat to be alone, although others seek company.

Elijah went far away from the crowds, into a desert, on his own. God provided a broom tree for him to rest under. Some translations call it a juniper tree. It was probably a shrub with small leaves that provided little shade, but in the heat of the desert any shade is welcome and offers rest.

When troubles fill our minds, going to a beautiful place, preferably outside, can help us to restore perspective. It can remind us that God, the creator of beauty, is still there, and he is our shelter. Beauty can move us from focusing on the immediate pressures to thinking about God. We are not told that Elijah prayed before running away; it was when he rested under the tree that he started to pray.

Elijah took a retreat by going off alone into the silence of the desert, leaving even his servant behind. In the desert he was away from distractions and surrounded by the natural world. In the stillness, he spoke to God and then he rested.

Sleep

After Elijah told God he had had enough and wanted to die, he lay down and slept. He seemed to fall asleep quickly in this quiet place. Then he woke and then slept again. A good sleep can make everything seem a bit easier. On the other hand, when we feel overtired, everything can feel overwhelming. During stressful times, we might need to sleep more than usual, but we might also find it harder to sleep. See chapter 4 for tips on improving sleep.

Touch

An angel touched Elijah. This happened twice (vv. 5, 7). Jesus also touched people, or allowed them to touch him, including those who were thought to be 'untouchable' or unclean (Matthew 9:20; Luke 7:37–38; 8:54). Touch can help us during difficult times, reassuring us that we are not alone and that someone cares.

Parents are advised to have skin-to-skin contact with their baby. Research suggests that touch helps infants to thrive, and a lack of touch is linked with failure to do so.[50] Touch has been found to be beneficial for adults as well as for children. Hugs from a partner may reduce blood pressure.[51] Massage can reduce a sense of pain.[52]

Some cultures and some personalities like touch more than others. We should respect people's boundaries. Some people give themselves 'butterfly hugs' as a way of comforting themselves after trauma, or calming themselves down when they feel upset.[53] Others find comfort through cuddling a baby or stroking a pet. Still others pray that God will touch them in a special way. He can still send angels to touch us, just as he did with Elijah.

Eating well

The angel gave Elijah bread and water. Shortly before this, Elijah had been fed meat brought to him by ravens (1 Kings 17:6). Jews considered ravens to be unclean birds. Elijah was fed meat out of their mouths – worms, perhaps? It was a miraculous provision, but maybe not what we would wish for.

This time, however, God sent Elijah an angel to personally bake bread for him while he slept. Hot, freshly baked bread appears a lot more appetising than cold bread. The smell is enough to start saliva flowing, even when stress has caused you to lose your appetite. In the UK, supermarkets pipe the smell of fresh bread through the store, to make people feel hungry and buy more. People are advised to bake bread when trying to sell their house, as the smell is thought to make viewers more likely to want to buy the house. Elijah smelled the hot bread, and he ate, and he drank the water that was also provided. Then he slept, then ate and drank again to give him strength for his journey.

Exercise

The passage tells us that Elijah travelled for 40 days and 40 nights to Horeb, the mountain of God. This was probably a journey of about 200 miles, so that would be an average of five miles per day (although some people think that '40 days and 40 nights' is symbolic and represents a long period of time). Elijah had run for his life towards the desert. He was probably still on foot, walking by now, rather than on an animal. It would have been possible for him to finish his 200-mile journey more quickly, although travelling was hard work in a rocky desert, especially if he needed to find food and water along the way. Elijah gave himself time. That time might have helped him start to recover from his depression.

This exercise wasn't a one-off for Elijah. On the last day of his earthly life he walked from Gilgal to Bethel to Jericho and across the River Jordan (2 Kings 2:1–8). That was probably at least 40 miles, which is not bad for an older man, even though it is mostly downhill.

Telling the story

God asked Elijah, 'What are you doing here, Elijah?' (v. 9). Elijah told him his story, saying he had been very zealous. He reported that the Israelites had rejected God and killed the prophets; Elijah was the only one left, and now they were trying to kill him, too. Four verses later, we read that God asked Elijah again, 'What are you doing here, Elijah?' Elijah told his story a second time, using exactly the same words he used shortly before.

Why did God ask Elijah the same thing twice? Had he forgotten what Elijah said? Wasn't he listening the first time? Perhaps God knew that Elijah could benefit from telling his story more than once. Often when we are going through a difficult time, we benefit from talking about what is happening, and our thoughts and feelings about it, and we may need to do this more than once. Research indicates that telling our stories can lead to physical health benefits and help us feel better emotionally, too.[54] Confessing our sins to others, as well as to God, can have similar benefits, taking away our sense of isolation and guilt and leading to restoration.

Sharing our story can help at times of stress. Sometimes this is called 'debriefing'.[55] Sharing our lives with others (during both good and challenging times) can help us to thrive and grow even stronger in our spiritual life, as well as deepening our relationships with other people, which makes us more resilient. If there is no one nearby with whom we can share our story, we might be able to communicate by phone or via the internet, or else to journal or blog about our thoughts and feelings. We also benefit from making time to reflect and talk to God about how we are feeling and the way life seems to be going. Like Elijah, we may need to share the same story more than once.

Support

Elijah told God, 'I am the only one left' (vv. 10, 14). He felt isolated and that he was the only person left in the whole of Israel who had not rejected God. He thought that he was about to be killed and so his ministry (and life) had been a waste of time, completely fruitless as there would be no one left who followed God. In effect, he was saying, 'My whole life as a prophet has been worthless.' He might have been descending into anger and self-pity.

God responded by telling Elijah to delegate tasks. Elijah was told to anoint Hazael and Jehu as kings to protect the people, and to anoint Elisha to succeed him as prophet. Elijah thought that the ministry would die with him, but God showed him that Elisha would continue the work.

God also pointed out that Elijah was not the only believer left – there were 7,000 who had not turned to Baal. Elijah's quiet ministry over the years had born more fruit than the spectacular ministry at Mount Carmel, where fire came down from heaven. Sometimes we don't see the fruit of our ministry, but God does.

Still, small voice: the sound of silence

Elijah went to Mount Horeb, which was a holy place, known as the 'mountain of God' (v. 8). This is where God had appeared to Moses in the burning bush (Exodus 3:1–2). It is also where Moses had struck a rock and water had flowed out for the Israelites (Exodus 17:6). It seems that God gave Moses the ten commandments at Horeb,[56] while fire blazed out of the mountain.

Elijah took a retreat to a holy place. Christians today sometimes speak of going to 'thin places' to retreat. This is a Celtic Christian term for places where heaven seems very close to earth, places soaked in prayer, where it seems easier to hear from God. Elijah might have come to this place because he wanted a powerful manifestation of God. Perhaps he expected God to be in the wind again, like the breath at creation (Genesis 2:7) or the wind in the time of Moses that brought the plague of locusts (Exodus 10:13) or the wind that 'went out from the Lord and drove quail in from the sea' (Numbers 11:31). Perhaps he thought God would make the earth tremble, like he had done at the same place when he gave the ten commandments (Exodus 19:18). Or maybe he was expecting more fire – like the fire that had burned the sacrifice on Mount Carmel, and the fire of the burning bush and the ten commandments.

But God does not always do what we tell him to do, or behave in the way we expect. Sometimes he does something new. This time, God was not in the wind, the earthquake or the fire. Instead, God came in a gentle whisper: a still, small voice, or the sound of silence. That is how God often speaks. If our lives are full of busyness and noise, it can be hard to hear the whisper.

I might have expected God to speak straight away when Elijah ran for his life. Instead, he began by meeting Elijah's basic needs for sleep, water, food and touch. It was only when these needs had been met, and Elijah had gone into a cave at the holy mountain, that God spoke. Meeting his physical needs was an important start, bringing him to a place where he was able to hear God speak, but it was not sufficient. Elijah was still hiding in a cave, fearing death. God did not give up on him. When Elijah's physical needs had been met, God spoke in the silence. This was the core of rebuilding Elijah's resilience.

Recommissioning

After a traumatic time, people tend to feel better if they are able to do something to help someone else. However small our act, it helps us to move on. We want to have purpose. God gave Elijah a new commission, to anoint and mentor Elisha. It was to be a fresh start. Elijah felt that he had been a failure as a prophet, because there was no fruit, but God recommissioned him for his new task, mentoring a younger man to take on the work after him. Such a recommissioning can lift our spirits, showing that there is still work to be done and that we can hand tasks over to a younger person and mentor them to continue the job.

The most significant parts of our life are generally our relationships with God and with others, and our having a meaningful purpose. God helped restore all of these for Elijah. God spoke and gave Elijah a new reason to live, a new calling and a new purpose. Immediately, Elijah stopped hiding. He overcame his fear of death, got out of the cave and went and found Elisha. We hear no more of Elijah's fear. The situation had not changed, but after hearing the gentle whisper of God, Elijah's resilience was restored. He went out and had a fruitful new season, mentoring Elisha.

Elijah is held up in the New Testament as an example of a man of faith whose prayers could stop or start the rain, and we are encouraged to pray like him (James 5:17–18). But when Elijah's prayer was not in keeping with God's plan, God did not say 'Yes'. Elijah had prayed that God would let him die. God never agreed to that. At the end of his life, God took Elijah up to heaven in a chariot of fire and a whirlwind (2 Kings 2:11). This time the wind and the fire did take Elijah to God. The name Elijah means 'My God is Yahweh'. Elijah did not get everything right, but he knew his God, and that is what matters most.

In summary, the acronym 'stress' reminds us of some of the building blocks of resilience that we can learn from Elijah. The physical factors are very evident, but other aspects of resilience are also present:

Sleep
Touch, and tell your story
Rest and retreat
Eat well, and exercise
Support
Still, small voice

Questions

1   Think about the areas discussed in this chapter – sleep; touch; telling your story; rest and retreat; eating well; exercise; support; and hearing God's still, small voice. Which of these do you think you should work on? What change can you make?

2   Is there someone you can share your story with this week?

3   If God called your name and asked, 'What are you doing here?', what would you reply?

4   Do you feel that you need more support? Can you do something about this? Have you prayed that God would open your eyes to see those who could support you – maybe not 7,000, but perhaps a few?

5   Does your daily schedule make you look like a person who wants to hear God's voice? How much time do you spend in silence, listening to God?

6

Emotional aspects of resilience

Some people imagine that to be resilient you must somehow rise above your emotions and not be influenced by them. This is not the case. Resilient people can be aware of and accept their emotions and find healthy ways of coping with them.

Among Christians, there is a tendency to believe that 'good Christians' never feel low, anxious, frustrated or angry, because they are always full of the joy of the Lord. The reality is that Christians have feelings just like anyone else, and it is what we do with the feelings that matters. The Bible does not tell us not to be angry; it says, '"In your anger do not sin": do not let the sun go down while you are still angry' (Ephesians 4:26). Just as we do not accept the health-and-wealth 'prosperity gospel', so we should not accept the 'gospel of emotional prosperity', which pretends that Christians can be free from negative feelings. Jesus was 'a man of suffering' (Isaiah 53:3), who wept in grief (John 11:35) and experienced anguish (Luke 22:44). If we are aware of the troubles in the world, then we will have times of sorrow and grief.

It is a normal human response that in periods of stress we experience negative emotions or stress-related symptoms. People who recognise that this is normal, and who take healthy steps to help themselves feel better, tend to get over their difficulties sooner. Those who tell themselves that they should not be feeling this way, or who berate themselves for not 'coping better', are at risk of becoming depressed about feeling depressed, or anxious about feeling anxious, thereby maintaining and worsening their symptoms.[57] Pushing emotions down and refusing to acknowledge them over a long period of time can lead to physical health problems.[58]

While a less resilient person might often say, 'I can't cope', the resilient person is unlikely to say this and will take life in their stride. Resilient people are usually seen by others as calm and emotionally stable, and not unduly distressed by minor events. The resilient person can tolerate other people and the frustration caused by interactions, without having meltdowns or unreasonable outbursts of anger.

Psychologists describe different ways of coping with stress and difficulty. They describe one coping style as 'emotion-focused coping'. This refers to ways of managing negative emotional responses to stress. We will list examples of this. They are not listed in order of importance. Different people will relate more to different examples.

Disclosing feelings (writing or talking)

Disclosing our feelings by writing or talking about them may bring a sense of relief. James Pennebaker has conducted many research studies in which he asked volunteers to write down their thoughts and feelings about stressful events they had experienced. Compared with volunteers who did not write about their feelings, these participants have shown improvements in their psychological and physical health – for example, an increase in their white blood cell count, indicating improved immunity, and fewer GP visits in the following six months.[59] Disclosing both the facts and the feelings was found to have more health benefits than just disclosing the facts.[60] Some people use a journal, a blog or poetry to write about their feelings.

Although it is beneficial to write about stressful events, it appears to be even more beneficial to talk about them.[61] Many people find it helpful to talk to friends, family members or a church leader about difficulties.

In chapter 5 we read about God asking Elijah, 'What are you doing here?', and Elijah ranting his story, twice. There are also other examples in the Bible of people feeling better after telling their stories. For example, a woman who had been bleeding for twelve years touched Jesus and was healed (Mark 5:27–29). She had tried to be anonymous in a crowd. As she had problems with menstruation, according to the Jewish teaching of the day she should not have been in the crowd at all. She was considered unclean, and was not meant to be near other people, because she would make them unclean when others in the crowd bumped into her. So why did Jesus ask who touched him, and draw attention to this woman who was trying to go unnoticed?

Jesus knew that by allowing her to tell her story, she could receive not only physical healing, but also emotional and social healing. Otherwise no one else would have known that she was healed, so she would still have been treated like an outcast. Jesus also brought spiritual healing through his words, 'Daughter, your faith has healed you. Go in peace' (Mark 5:34).

Another example of Jesus letting people tell their story is his conversation with two disciples on the Emmaus Road, after his resurrection (Luke 24:13–35). These disciples were downcast, talking about the death of Jesus. Jesus came alongside them and listened to their story. Why didn't he tell them straight away that he was alive? He could have ended their sorrow sooner, and saved them a long walk to Emmaus and then straight back to Jerusalem. Instead, Jesus let them tell their story of trauma and loss before he revealed who he was. Perhaps it was important for them to tell their story and process their grief before they were ready to move on.

Praying and lamenting

As well as talking to other people, we can talk to God about our situation and feelings, and pray for help and strength. Some people find that writing a prayer journal helps them to focus their prayers.

Reading the psalms in the Bible can help us to find words that resonate with our feelings, and remind us that God is big enough to cope with all our emotions, including anger. The books of Lamentations and Job also show us how we can express our feelings. Many people have found it helpful to write poems or psalms of lament, to express grief.[62] Putting our feelings into words helps us to acknowledge those feelings and to take them to God.

Wilson and Wilson state:

> There's something about expressing what we feel in words, and music, that helps us to come to terms with it, and to take it before God in anguished prayer. Christians, in particular, can feel like we ought not to vent our emotions at God; we prefer tidy prayers like 'God we don't understand, but we trust you' to the chaotic, confused, howling prayers we find in the Psalms. But those songs are in the Bible because we are supposed to express ourselves that way. 'How long, O Lord? Will you forget us forever? What are you *doing*?... If you ever loved us, O God, come and fix things. Now!' If God is big enough to be worth yelling at about your situation, he is big enough to take your pain, hear your lament and somehow use it to comfort you in the confusion... Lament, you see, is about bringing your sorrows to God, in painful description, petition and confusion, and throwing all your doubts and questions at him. Rushing to dump them on friends, on family or on Facebook, without having gone to God with them first, is not lamenting but venting, and in the long run it doesn't do nearly so much good.[63]

Giving anxieties to God

We are encouraged to bring all our anxieties and cares to Jesus (1 Peter 5:7). Jesus taught us to trust God and not worry about our clothes or our food, or about the future in general (Matthew 6:25–34). It can be very helpful to meditate on the words of Jesus and to choose to trust God whatever happens to us. *The Message* paraphrases part of Jesus' teaching on this in the following beautiful manner, which can soothe our troubled souls:

> Give your entire attention to what God is doing right now, and don't get worked up about what may or may not happen tomorrow. God will help you deal with whatever hard things come up when the time comes.
>
> MATTHEW 6:34 (MSG)

Corrie ten Boom certainly had reasons for anxiety, as she was sent to a concentration camp during World War II for hiding Jews. But her father had prepared her well to let go of worry. As a child, she had discovered the reality of death when she saw a dead baby. She then worried that her parents would also die one day. She recalls crying out to her father:

> 'I need you!' I sobbed. 'You can't die! You can't!'
>
> 'Corrie,' he began gently. 'When you and I go to Amsterdam, when do I give you your ticket?'
>
> 'Why, just before we get on the train.'
>
> 'Exactly. And our wise Father in heaven knows when we're going to need things, too. Don't run out ahead of him, Corrie. When the time comes that some of us will have to die, you will look into your heart and find the strength you need – just in time.'[64]

Although death and suffering are a reality, we do not need to be anxious, because God will give us what we need, just in time, if we trust him and turn to him. We might not feel resilient enough to cope with suffering, but God can provide the strength we need at the time.

> All you need to remember is that God will never let you down; he'll never let you be pushed past your limit; he'll always be there to help you come through it.
>
> 1 CORINTHIANS 10:13 (MSG)

Crying

Releasing pent-up emotions in a way that does not harm anyone is another form of emotion-focused coping. One way to do this is by allowing ourselves to cry. Crying is normal at times of stress or grief (even though some groups look down on it, and so sometimes the crying is done secretly). Crying is healthy, and people tend to feel better after crying. Researchers have analysed tears and found that emotional tears are chemically different from the tears caused by dirt in the eye or peeling an onion. It has been reported that emotional tears contain stress hormones. Crying, by eliminating the excess hormones, may relieve stress.[65]

Crying is endorsed in the Bible. We are told that there is a time to weep (Ecclesiastes 3:4), and Jesus himself wept (John 11:35). Jesus said, 'Blessed are you who weep' (Luke 6:21), and we read in Ecclesiastes 7:3 that 'crying is better than laughing. It blotches the face but it scours the heart' (MSG).

In Britain, there has traditionally been a culture of the 'stiff upper lip' – the belief that strong people never let their lip wobble and are never seen crying. But in reality, crying is not a weakness and, just because someone cries, it does not mean that they lack resilience. In fact, crying may help build our resilience, as we are likely to feel better afterwards.

Distraction and recreation

Another coping technique is to distract ourselves from stress or unpleasant feelings, such as a low mood or anxiety. Sometimes clients tell me sheepishly that they have been using distraction, as if that is a terrible thing. In fact, distraction can be a healthy and appropriate response at times, especially as a short-term coping response to acute stress. It is not necessarily sinful or unhelpful.

During times of pain, stress or trauma, sometimes we just need to survive and get through each hour until we have got over the worst and start to feel a bit better. For example, a woman in labour may be encouraged to choose something to listen to or watch to distract herself from the pain.

Avoid forms of distraction that are harmful, such as self-harm, excessive alcohol, driving unsafely (e.g. speeding, or driving under the influence of alcohol), or gambling or spending leading to significant debt. Excessive eating over a long period of time can lead to obesity, so this is another unadvisable form of distraction. But recreation that does not cause harm, done in moderation, can be a good choice to distract us from short-term pain or distress.

We can distract ourselves from worries by indulging our senses – savouring delicious fruit, smelling freshly cut grass, concentrating on beautiful music or looking at photographs. Activities we enjoy can help to lift our spirits.

Helpful recreational activities include reading, listening to music, playing sport, participating in a club, engaging in a hobby, cooking, gardening, doing craft activities and playing games. Socialising with friends can also be a helpful distraction from concerns, as can connecting with people on social media (as long as none of these activities are done to excess, preventing us from sleeping or functioning in everyday life). Of course, if we are distracting ourselves from something that we really need to face, or are procrastinating instead of getting on with necessary activities, then at some point we need to stop distracting ourselves and face the issue.

Relaxation and slow breathing

When we feel stressed, anxious or tired, it is good to plan activities that we find relaxing. This could include a long bath or swim, or something calming like meditation, colouring or gentle music. Some people find driving relaxing, and others bake or read to relax. Structured relaxation exercises can also be helpful – for example, clenching and then relaxing each muscle group in turn (perhaps starting with toes, and moving up to buttocks, stomach, fingers, shoulders, neck, lips and eyes). Examples of how to do this can be found through an online search for 'progressive muscular relaxation'.

Slow breathing from the stomach also helps us to relax, and this is especially important for people who suffer from panic and anxiety.[66] Concentrating on slowing down your breathing can help to calm racing thoughts. For other people, simply making time to rest may be all that is needed.

Avoiding negativity

Frequent grumbling, complaining, criticism and ruminating on negative thoughts can make us prone to depression.[67] Instead, we can be intentional about avoiding negativity and choose to be around positive people. We should seek to encourage people and build them up. As it says in Ephesians 4:29, 'Do not let any unwholesome talk come out of your mouths, but only what is helpful for building others up according to their needs, that it may benefit those who listen.'[68]

Seeking help

People who have ongoing problems with depression, anxiety, eating disorders, trauma, stress, self-hatred, low self-esteem or other mental health issues are advised to seek help from a health professional, such as a doctor, counsellor or psychologist, who may offer talking treatment, recommend medication or both. Part of the therapy may involve challenging negative thoughts and replacing them with more helpful ways of thinking, or looking for a positive sense of meaning in our situation. Whether we seek professional assistance or help ourselves (perhaps using a self-help book), the aim is to have emotional good health so that we can live life to the full, with God.

If we don't need therapy, we might still benefit from talking to someone who can ask us questions that help us reflect – for example, a spiritual director, mentor, life coach, debriefer, supervisor or friend. Taking steps to help ourselves grow is a sign of strength, not weakness.

Smiling and laughing

The suggestions above focus on finding ways to cope with negative emotions. Another strategy is to focus on producing a positive emotional state. Haglund and colleagues report that 'resilient individuals are often characterised by positive emotions such as positive attitude, optimism, and sense of humor'.[69]

Professor Stephen Hawking, who lived with motor neurone disease, said at the BBC Reith lecture in January 2016, 'It's also important not to become angry, no matter how difficult life may seem, because you can lose all hope if you can't laugh at yourself and life in general.'[70]

A series of experiments have demonstrated that the simple act of smiling can improve mood and reduce stress. For example, in one study, 170 participants were asked to perform two mildly stressful tasks while holding chopsticks in their mouths. Some were asked to hold the chopsticks in a manner that pushed their mouths into a smile, while others were asked to hold them in a way that caused a neutral expression. The smiling participants were found to have lower heart rates during stress recovery than the neutral group, showing that the simple act of smiling had physiological benefits.[71]

It is often reported that people in the emergency services use black humour (humour about sad situations) to help them remain resilient when dealing with difficult events. But the humour does not have to be black. Barrett and Martin point out that people in extreme environments, such as those aboard nuclear submarines, astronauts or those on an Antarctic base, are often prolific pranksters who cope with fear and boredom by playing practical jokes.[72]

A 15-year follow-up study of 53,556 people found that a higher rating for the cognitive component of humour was associated with a reduced risk of death from any cause among women, and a reduced risk of death from infections among men.[73] Laughter relaxes the body, and it may boost the immune system, increase tolerance of pain and trigger the release of endorphins, leaving us feeling more positive.[74] Laughter also strengthens relationships, and it keeps us focused on the present moment. It is difficult to feel anxious, sad or angry when we are genuinely laughing. After a good laugh we often feel refreshed and find that we have a new perspective.

It can be worthwhile seeking out humour – for example, by looking for funny shows, books or movies, as well as spending time around people who are fun. Asking people to share funny stories, and sharing some of our own, can also help us feel better. Trying an activity that we are bad at (perhaps Russian dancing) can be another way to help us laugh at ourselves. Some people even choose to simulate laughter (for example, at a laughter therapy group), which can feel so bizarre that it often leads to genuine laughter. Choosing to laugh about frustrating situations, such as travel delays, our own mistakes or poor service in a restaurant, instead of complaining about them can significantly improve our mood. Children laugh more than adults, so spending time playing with children can be another way to boost laughter.

Building resilience in children: emotional health

Children need to know that they are loved. They need to be given time, attention and affection from their caregivers. They need to be listened to and reassured if they are worried. Love and attention will help the child to feel confident. The poem 'Children learn what they live', by Dorothy Law Nolte,[75] reminds us of the importance of creating the right emotional environment for children.

It should be natural to have fun with children and laugh with them. When a child cries, we can try to find out what is the matter and to comfort them, instead of telling them not to cry. Children should be encouraged to share their feelings with an adult they trust who can help them.

The Christian music group Fischy Music have a range of great songs that promote resilience, including 'Sing to make you feel good', which affirms the physical and emotional benefits of singing; 'Bag of worries', which encourages the sharing of worries; 'My old friend tears', which tells us that tears can be a friend; and 'Bring it all to me', which teaches us to share all our emotions with God.[76]

Some children have significant difficulties with anxiety, grief, depression, anger or other emotional issues. Professional help should be sought in such cases.

Linking back to spiritual factors: cultivating contentment

As mentioned in chapter 4, the apostle Paul wrote that he had 'learned to be content whatever the circumstances' (Philippians 4:11). We can try to learn this, too. Embracing simplicity and choosing not to overcomplicate things may be part of this.

Studying what else Paul wrote in Philippians can give us clues to what his secret of contentment might have been; most of these are qualities that we have already discussed. Even when he was writing from a prison cell, Paul practised prayer, gratitude, hope and looking at the bigger, eternal perspective. He had a sense of purpose (1:24–26) and trusted God to provide the strength he needed (4:13). He taught that we should not complain or argue (2:14; 4:2) but should live lives of love (2:2–4) and choose to rejoice in the Lord (3:1; 4:4, 10). He also taught us to meditate on things that are true and lovely (4:8).

Deep contentment comes from a deep spiritual life, and this is what we should nourish. We know from the book of Acts that Paul worshipped God by singing even during the night in a prison cell (Acts 16:25). Elsewhere, Paul prays that believers will be 'filled to the measure of all the fullness of God' (Ephesians 3:19). We can pray this for ourselves and for others. If we are filled to the measure with the fullness of God, we will know the fruit of the Holy Spirit in our lives – 'love, joy, peace, forbearance, kindness, goodness, faithfulness, gentleness and self-control' (Galatians 5:22–23). These qualities bring contentment.

Paul ends his letter to the Philippians with a blessing: 'Receive and experience the amazing grace of the Master, Jesus Christ, deep, deep within yourselves' (Philippians 4:23, MSG). Having a deep knowledge of the grace of Jesus brings us a sense of contentment and helps us to cope with whatever life may throw at us.

In Psalm 131:2 we see a beautiful picture of contentment:

> I have calmed and quietened myself,
>> I am like a weaned child with its mother;
>> like a weaned child I am content.

David, the psalmist, however, was not always calm. As we will see in the next chapter, David was no stranger to emotion, and to emotional aspects of resilience.

Questions

1 How is your emotional health? Is there anything that would help improve it?

2 What do you do when you feel sad, anxious or angry? Is this a helpful response or do you think there might be a better strategy you could try?

3 Can you share a funny story with someone, or find an opportunity to laugh today?

4 Do you think you are a contented person? If not, what might help you to be more content?

5 How can we help others, including children, to deal with negative emotions and be emotionally resilient?

7

Resilience in the life of David

David was another leader who suffered many trials and tribulations as God prepared him for the work ahead. Although described by God as 'a man after my own heart' (Acts 13:22; see also 1 Samuel 13:14), he was far from perfect, and he experienced many ups and downs – some of his own making and some as a result of the malice of others. In particular, during his early years he was the object of King Saul's wrath, and he had to flee for his life into the desert. Those years on the run in the wilderness were perhaps the most formative of his life. Many of his psalms were written during that period.

David the man

David was charismatic, a natural leader, a man around whom others spontaneously gathered. Even as a shepherd boy out on the hills he showed exceptional courage, taking on lions and bears to protect his flock (1 Samuel 17:34–36). When Goliath challenged the armies of Israel, it was David who bravely stepped forward and felled the giant with only his sling as a weapon (1 Samuel 17:41–50). His continuing success against the Philistines brought him great popularity (1 Samuel 18:6–7) as well as incurring the jealous anger of Saul.

David was far more than a soldier, however. He was a warrior with the heart of a poet, a sensitive soul who was deeply devoted to God.

Musically gifted, he loved to play his harp and compose songs. When Saul suffered bouts of mental anguish, it was David's playing that lifted his mood (1 Samuel 16:14–23). In his own times of darkness, David used his gift to turn his heart towards God, and we benefit from his legacy in the book of Psalms, more than 70 of which bear his name.

It would be easy to think that David was naturally resilient, able to cope easily with whatever adversity came his way. Certainly, he had a high threshold for coping with trouble and a huge capacity for bouncing back after setbacks, but even David had limitations. In 1 Samuel 30, we find David facing perhaps the darkest day of his life. This one incident will be the focus of our attention as we seek to learn the secret of David's resilience.

David's darkest day

David had been on the run from Saul for a long time, and in his desperation had found an unlikely hiding place among the Philistines with King Achish (1 Samuel 27:1–4). By carefully creating the impression that he was now on their side, David found favour with Achish until one day some of the leading Philistine commanders objected to his presence, fearing he would betray them. Reluctantly, Achish had to let David go, so he and his men returned to their base in the desert stronghold of Ziklag, a long three-day trek through the wilderness.

A shocking scene of devastation awaited them on their arrival home. During their absence a group of Amalekite raiders had attacked the settlement and burned it to the ground. Worse still, they had taken captive all the people. Their wives and children had been taken hostage. Already tired from the journey, and weary after many months of fighting, these battle-hardened warriors broke down and wept as they encountered the scene and considered their loss. With characteristic Jewish abandonment (no British reserve here), we read that 'David and his men wept aloud until they had no strength left to weep' (v. 4).

Grown men crying

We have seen already that there is nothing shameful about crying, although many men consider it a sign of weakness. Boys are often brought up with the adage that 'big boys don't cry', suggesting that to be upset is a denial of true masculinity. In many societies, it is considered better not to express such 'negative' emotion in public. Yet here David's men showed no such restraint. They were not afraid of expressing their emotions, of giving vent to their feelings. Confronted by such a tragedy, it is only natural to be overwhelmed by grief and loss, and tears bring their own healing. David was also affected, shedding his own tears. His two wives (Ahinoam and Abigail) had been taken too, and he shared the pain of his men as they faced this trauma together (vv. 4–5).

Trauma

Schaefer and Schaefer define trauma as 'any serious event that threatens or affects the life or physical integrity of a person, or loved one. Experiencing, witnessing, or becoming aware of such an event creates intense fear, helplessness, or horror in the affected person.'[77] Trauma has a seismic impact, shaking a person's deepest convictions, and raising questions for them, such as 'Why me?' and 'Where is God in this?' The shock and scale of such events have the potential to destabilise even hardy individuals and knock them completely off balance.

It is easy to see why the events at Ziklag can justifiably be described as traumatic. Not only did David and his men experience the unexpected plunder of their possessions and destruction of their property by the violent actions of others, but they also had no idea what had happened to their families. Had the women been raped or tortured? Had the children been harmed? Were they dead, or had they been taken hostage? Such major uncertainty multiplied their pain and anxiety.

Anger

As is common with grief, anger is never too far from the surface and quite soon David's men could contain themselves no longer. They needed someone to blame for what had happened, and their fury turned towards David, the obvious choice. Once loyal and obedient troops now took their frustration out on their leader: 'The men were talking of stoning him; each one was bitter in spirit because of his sons and daughters' (v. 6). They were unable to make sense of what had happened, and the cauldron of their emotions spilled over into a bitter attack. Many leaders will have seen this dynamic at work. When people's dreams are shattered, their hurt is often transferred to those in leadership over them. Counsellors will have felt it too when those in pain vent their fury at them, even though they are only trying to help.

David's own distress was intensified as he saw those whom he had led and trusted now turning on him, and he feared for his safety. He could easily have retaliated out of his own hurt and confusion, but he chose not to do so. Instead, we read these remarkable words: 'But David found strength in the Lord his God' (v. 6).

Faith and resilience

Trauma is a very subjective thing. Two people facing the same circumstances may respond differently according to how they interpret what has happened to them. This seems to be the case here. David does not appear to have allowed his grief and anger to overwhelm him. While his men became bitter and turned against him, David chose a different response and turned to the Lord. His resilience seems to be rooted in his faith, and his deep spirituality helped him to manage both his thought life (the cognitive dimension) and his feelings (the emotional dimension) in a helpful way.

This faith-based response may be called spiritual resilience, and can be described as 'the capacity, when faced with adversity, to cope using religious resources'.[78] Over the years of knowing God, David had built an inner pathway that took him straight to God. His default position in a crisis was to turn to God for help. This had become a habitual response, a learned behaviour, and it is what enabled him to control his emotions and reactions in a moment of great pressure.

Building an inner pathway to God

Many sports people know the value of repeating basic skills over and over again until they become ingrained responses, or of practising set routines repeatedly until they are instinctive. The same is true for military personnel or people who work in the emergency services. The reason for this is that in the heat of the moment, when the pressure is on, we have little time to choose how to respond. Training has to take over so that we act almost without thinking. Spiritual disciplines provide the equivalent foundation for people of faith. The daily practices of prayer and worship, of Bible reading and fellowship with others, need to become second nature to us so that when we find ourselves facing major disruption, we are able to turn instinctively to God as David did. Kirsten Birkett, writing in the context of preparing ministers for the rigours of parish ministry, notes, 'We can be encouraged that a lot of what is recommended for building resilience for stressful lives and work places is already what most Christians will do daily anyway. The challenge is to do them more.'[79]

So, what exactly did David do in his moment of crisis, and how did he manage to strengthen himself in the Lord his God? We are not told exactly, but we can draw several inferences from what we know of David's normal response to adversity as reflected in the book of Psalms.

Step aside

The first significant factor is that he appears to have stepped aside from the immediate situation. This may have been for the sake of his safety, but also to give him time and space in which to think. No doubt removing himself physically from the source of his distress also enabled him to look at his predicament more objectively. This was not, however, escapism or denial. He stepped aside from people in order to be alone with God. This would seem to be a good practice to follow when we find ourselves becoming overwhelmed by our fears and worries. It enables us to regain perspective and to see things from God's vantage point.

Concept of God

David had already experienced God's power to deliver him when he faced Goliath, and his understanding of God is summed up in the expression 'the Lord his God' (v. 6). David enjoyed a deep personal relationship with God. He could say with confidence, 'I love you, Lord, my strength. The Lord is my rock, my fortress and my deliverer; my God is my rock, in whom I take refuge, my shield and the horn of my salvation, my stronghold' (Psalm 18:1–2). For David, this God was sovereign, the Lord in control of everything that was happening, even if it did not appear that way immediately. David's faith was being tested here, but he knew that God was still in charge of events. He believed that God would not fail him now. Trouble has a way of sifting out what we really believe about God. When the chips are down, we need to be firmly connected to a God whom we know to be the sovereign Lord. Any inadequate understanding of God will leave us exposed and vulnerable to despair, weakening our resilience.

The power of prayer

If we use our imaginations a little, we can paint a picture of what David may have done as he found solitude for a brief time in the desert. Almost certainly he would have prayed, crying from his heart to God for his help and deliverance. This would have been no wishy-washy, half-hearted monologue of vague piety, but a gut-wrenching shout to God for rescue. Many of David's early psalms reflect this passionate devotion: 'Answer me when I call to you, my righteous God. Give me relief from my distress; have mercy on me and hear my prayer' (Psalm 4:1). See also Psalms 5:1–3; 57:1; 61:1–3; 62:1–2, 5–8. We must be honest with God when we pray and get past the barrier of polite formalism that robs prayer of its efficacy. God wants us to be real with him.

Praise as a weapon

Knowing David's love of singing, I feel sure he would have lifted up his voice to God in praise, not because he felt like singing, but because he understood the power of praise. When we find ourselves in a tight corner, we can give expression to our faith by singing aloud, and this somehow releases the power of God into our situations. These words are typical of David's response to difficulty: 'But I will sing of your strength, in the morning I will sing of your love; for you are my fortress, my refuge in times of trouble. You are my strength, I sing praise to you; you, God, are my fortress, my God on whom I can rely' (Psalm 59:16–17). See also Psalms 7:17; 34:1–3; 59:9.

Honesty before God

David's relationship with God was based on being honest and real. He was not afraid to voice his complaint when he felt God was slow to act, or share his sadness when he was troubled. For this reason, many of the psalms that David wrote are classified as psalms of lament, sad songs that come from the heart and reflect a measure of pain. Sometimes David found himself questioning God. 'How long, Lord? Will you forget me for ever?', he cried on one occasion. 'How long will you hide your face from me?' (Psalm 13:1). Another time he revealed his despair to God: 'I am worn out from my groaning. All night long I flood my bed with weeping and drench my couch with tears. My eyes grow weak with sorrow; they fail because of all my foes' (Psalm 6:6–7). See also Psalms 3, 5, 6 and 22.

It is inconceivable that after the events at Ziklag, David did not express his true feelings to God. Being able to say exactly what we feel in prayer (or through journalling, painting or talking to another person) has a cathartic and healing effect on us. God is big enough to cope with whatever we want to say to him. Interestingly enough, almost all the psalms of lament that begin with anger or pain of some kind end up with expressions of trust in God. It seems we have to work through our emotions before we can move on. It never does us any good to suppress or deny our negative feelings.

Learning to trust

Another feature of David's relationship with God is his ability to trust God within the context of his pain and confusion. It is easy to trust God when all is going well, but what about when our backs are up against the wall? Writer Brennan Manning has said that what we most need in our lives is ruthless trust – ruthless because in order to trust God fully we must be free of self-pity. He writes, 'Unwavering trust is a rare and precious thing because it often demands a degree of courage that borders on the heroic… It requires heroic courage to trust in the love of God no matter what happens to us.'[80] So often David chose to trust in this way when everything was against him: 'When I am afraid, I put my trust in you. In God, whose word I praise – in God I trust and am not afraid. What can mere mortals do to me?' (Psalm 56:3–4). See also Psalms 4:8; 13:5–6; 27:1–3; 56:10–11; 57:2–3.

I imagine David surveying the ruins of Ziklag and somehow bravely choosing to trust in God, whom he knew to be faithful, even though at that moment trust did not come easily to him. He must have faced the battle that we all face from time to time – to go with what we see with our eyes (the facts) or what we know in our hearts (that God is faithful); to choose to walk not by sight but by faith in God (2 Corinthians 5:7).

Strength to carry on

As he thought and prayed, worshipped and offered himself again to God, David began to find his strength returning. This was a supernatural impartation that happens whenever we choose to lean hard upon God. Isaiah the prophet said that those who wait upon the Lord will renew their strength (Isaiah 40:31), and from somewhere deep within himself David found the resolve to keep going. This is a dimension of resilience that is available to people of faith. We do not have to keep going in our own strength. We can follow David's pattern of response when we find ourselves in crisis. God will share his own strength with us when we are humble enough to ask for his divine assistance.

Seeking counsel

There is one more thing that David did before he returned to action. He consulted with Abiathar the priest, seeking to discern the will of God when it came to making a response (vv. 7–8). This is such a wise thing to do. Not only do we need relational support in times of need, but sometimes we need the help of experienced people with expertise and insight. David took Abiathar along with him because he valued his pastoral support and spiritual insight. We can all benefit from such people – be it a pastor, counsellor, mentor, coach, spiritual director or wise friend. There is no need to go it alone and think that we have to have all the answers ourselves. Seeking advice is a sign of wisdom, not weakness, and resilient people make sure they have trusted people to turn to when they need help. Together, David and Abiathar concluded that it would be right to pursue the Amalekites.

Eugene Peterson brilliantly sums up this passage of scripture and the process we have been talking about:

> David prayed; David worshipped; David called on his pastor, Abiathar, for counsel. David went deep within himself, met God, and found strength and direction to stride into the way of salvation. As his exterior world collapsed, he returned to the interior, rebuilt his primary identity, recovered his base. David and Abiathar came out of the place of quietness and counsel with a plan.[81]

Here is as good a formula for resilience as we could wish for, but it does require that we have done the prior work of laying down in our hearts a pathway to God. If it is not our instinctive response to turn to God in times of need, when trouble comes it will be too late. In the panic that accompanies catastrophe we will be all at sea. Only if we have trained ourselves in the disciplines of dependency will we be able to stand our ground when everything around us is shaking.

Growing through pain

Not everything about trauma is negative. Indeed, it has become common to refer to the positive changes that can take place after trauma as post-traumatic growth. Changes may take place in how we see ourselves and our relationships, and how we understand God, the world, or life's purpose and meaning. Often people who have been through trauma feel they are more understanding of others, less judgemental and more accepting, perhaps more compassionate and empathetic. As David and his men set off in pursuit of the Amalekites, David shows evidence of such a change himself.

First, he allowed those of his men who were not yet fully recovered to stay behind, one third of his army (vv. 9–10). Then, when they came across a wandering Egyptian, they showed him compassion and provided him with food and water. This surprising act of kindness, in fact, was the key to David finding the Amalekites, for the stranger (unknown to them) had been part of their army and could lead them to where they were camped (vv. 11–15).

So it was that David and his men fell upon the Amalekites by surprise, and recovered everything that was taken from them: 'Nothing was missing: young or old, boy or girl, plunder or anything else they had taken. David brought everything back' (v. 19). On their return to Ziklag, David ensured that those men who had not gone with them received their share of the plunder (vv. 21–25). Furthermore, he generously sent presents from the plunder to those who had been his friends and allies during his time in the wilderness (vv. 26–31). Although scripture does not make this point, could we say that the plunder represents for us the good that comes out of our times of adversity, the kind of growth about which we have spoken?

Happy endings?

Not every story has such a happy ending. The purpose of the account is not to guarantee us unconditional happiness but to remind us that even in extreme adversity we can still find our strength in God. Some stories may not end quite as well, but the lesson is still important – the spiritual dimension to our lives can become a major factor in our emotional resilience. The daily disciplines of devotion may not always feel significant at the time, but each day, whether or not we realise it, we are building the inner pathway to God that will equip us well for coping when hard times come. As Kirsten Birkett says, 'Overall, it is the cumulative effect of genuine deepening spirituality that would seem to be the best way to prepare for stress, in a way that will enable one to come back from it even stronger.'[82]

Questions

1 How easy do you find it to be honest with God about your emotions?

2 How are you building a pathway to God in your life? Why is this an important factor in building resilience?

3 Review the different steps David may have taken in order to strengthen himself in God. What can you learn from his example?

4 Who might be an Abiathar to you? Is there someone you can turn to for wise counsel in a time of crisis?

5 Try writing your own psalm, expressing your feelings (positive or negative).

8

Cognitive and creative aspects of resilience

'Cognitive' refers to anything connected with thinking or conscious mental processes. In this chapter we will discuss a number of cognitive aspects of resilience, including problem-solving; maintaining active thinking during crises; avoiding rumination; mental flexibility; lifelong learning and expertise; our beliefs about difficult events and the sense of meaning we create; our theology of suffering; challenging unhelpful thoughts; choosing to focus on biblical truths; and asking God for wisdom, discernment and inspiration. We will also discuss the role of creativity and imagination.

Problem-solving

In chapter 6 we considered emotion-focused coping. Another coping style that is often employed is 'problem-focused coping'. This involves tackling problems by dealing with the root cause. This might include implementing better time management, asking for practical help or following problem-solving steps. Problem-solving is one example of a cognitive process.

Some people are naturally good at problem-solving, and come up with solutions without even realising they are doing it. Other people struggle to think of effective solutions to difficulties or believe there is no way out of their situation. Poor problem-solving skills are associated with feelings of hopelessness, angry outbursts and suicide attempts. Training people in problem-solving skills has been shown to be an effective mental health intervention.[83]

Problem-solving can be divided into six straightforward steps:

1 Identify the problem as soon as possible.
2 Define the problem accurately.
3 Think of as many solutions as possible. Write them all down and do not censor any, as they may lead on to better ideas.
4 List the pros and cons of each solution.
5 Select the best solution or combination of solutions.
6 Try the solution and then evaluate how it went.[84]

This is not the only method possible for solving problems, but it is one effective and well-known method.

One particular type of problem that may need to be addressed is conflict.[85] The Bible provides some principles for conflict resolution,[86] but it can take a lot of thinking, prayer and planning to do this well. Trying to see things from someone else's perspective can be one helpful principle, and following the problem-solving steps can help identify solutions that we can implement with an attitude of grace.

Problem-solving can help us deal with all sorts of issues, from the small (such as how to spend a day off) to the big (such as where to live, or whether to evacuate from a country facing civil war). Asking God to guide us as we problem-solve is important, especially when making important decisions.

Camilla Carr and Jon James were held as hostages for 14 months in Chechnya. While in captivity, they problem-solved whether to try to escape and decided that it was too risky. So they problem-solved how to spend their time when they had no freedom and little room. As well as trying to exercise and meditate, they decorated their small space with bits of dry orange peel and made their own games with whatever they could find, including used matches and Blu-Tack.[87] Even when it might look like we have no options, it may be possible to find a way to make things better.

Keeping an active mind during crises

Remaining with the theme of resilient hostages, we can consider Terry Waite. Waite was taken hostage in Beirut and held for nearly five years; for nearly four of those years he was kept in solitary confinement. Yet he has claimed that he was not completely captive, because his mind could take him out of his captivity. He used his mind to think about his family, to pray, to mentally write his autobiography and to focus on pleasant memories. He requested books, and read those he was brought (although he felt disappointed when the only book in English that a guard could find for him was a breastfeeding manual with no illustrations).[88]

One woman I debriefed was a victim in an armed robbery, and coped very well. When we discussed what had helped her cope, she described thinking during the robbery about how she was going to hide her wedding ring from the thieves. Filling her mind with plans, instead of thinking about her fears or helplessness, helped her come out of the situation in good psychological health. Maintaining a sense of hope instead of helplessness, remaining mentally active and continuing to pray for God to help us can make us resilient under pressure.

Avoiding rumination

Although it is good to keep an active and focused mind during a crisis, rumination should be avoided. Ruminating refers to going over the same (usually negative) thoughts again and again without coming up with any solutions. This is not helpful, and is associated with increased risk of anxiety and depression.

Mental flexibility

Mental flexibility is important, as plans often need to be changed. Resilient people are able to cope with change and come up with a plan B, and perhaps plans C, D and E.

Lifelong learning and expertise

Intelligence and knowledge can help us to anticipate and plan ahead, and also to find good solutions to difficulties, perhaps based on previous experience. Increasing our knowledge base can help us make better decisions.

Resilient people see all experiences as opportunities to learn. We learn what helps us cope in stressful situations, and what does not. Being well equipped, briefed and trained puts us in the best position to deal with difficulties. Role-play, practice and simulation exercises can be especially helpful, particularly for preparing us to cope in insecure environments or traumatic incidents. We can develop our mental toughness.

Studying how other people have dealt with challenges makes us more likely to have ideas of ways we might be able to face challenges ourselves. For example, reading testimonies about how people have stayed close to God during difficult times can help build our faith and prepare us for challenges we might face. And reading about resilience may give us ideas of ways to build our resilience!

Our beliefs about traumatic events, and the sense of meaning we create

The meaning that we give to difficult events and the way we think about them (i.e. our appraisal of the events) influence how we cope.[89] People who conclude that a traumatic event was their fault, happened because God was punishing them or occurred because the world is meaningless tend to cope less well than those who conclude that both good and bad things happen and the trauma was not their fault. People who believe that good can come out of suffering (see Romans 8:28), or who use challenges to produce growth in their lives, cope better than those who believe that they will be miserable forever because of what they have experienced. Focusing on helping others can enable us to cope with suffering ourselves.[90]

Joni Eareckson Tada has experienced more suffering than most people. She was paralysed by a diving accident as a teenager in 1967 and has been unable to move her hands or legs since. In more recent years she has battled with cancer as well as chronic pain. While in hospital after her accident, Joni made the decision not to waste her suffering, but to see her situation as, in her words, 'a gymnasium for my soul, a proving ground for my faith, and a mission field for God'.[91] Since then she has helped many thousands of people through her advocacy, writing and speaking engagements, often exploring questions related to suffering.[92]

Theology of suffering

As Christians, our theology of suffering will influence our appraisal of traumatic events. People who have never thought through their theology of suffering may struggle. For example, if I believe that God will physically protect me from all harm and then I am violently attacked, I will start to question why God did not protect me. Many people stop believing in God when they suffer – for example, after the death of a loved one or through personal illness or injury. They may be unable to believe that a God of love could allow suffering.

God has not promised to protect us from all physical harm. In fact, the Bible makes it clear that we can *expect* difficulties. Suffering happens, and we are likely to experience it. Jesus and his disciples went through deep suffering, and the apostle Paul experienced a breathtaking list of traumatic experiences (2 Corinthians 11:23–29). What we can hang on to is that God is merciful, and he will be with us in the difficulties, and when we enter into eternal life there will be an end to death, crying and pain (Revelation 21:4).

Job suffered more than I can imagine, but he was still able to say:

> I know that my redeemer lives,
>   and that in the end he will stand on the earth.
> And after my skin has been destroyed,
>   yet in my flesh I will see God.
> JOB 19:25–26

God chose never to answer Job's questions, and God never explained the reason for his suffering. If Job could show such faith even before Jesus lived on earth, then I hope that I can also trust God despite a lack of answers. Helen Roseveare was a missionary doctor in the Congo, who was captured by rebel soldiers during a civil war. She experienced great brutality. She believed that God asked her, 'Can you thank me for trusting you with this [suffering], even if I never tell you why?'[93]

If we are to survive suffering with our faith intact (or, even better, deepened), we need to continue to trust God even though he might not answer our prayers in the way that we want him to. It can help if we accept that we may never understand why God allows certain things to happen. It is common to go from thinking that we know all the answers to accepting the mystery that God's thoughts are not our thoughts, and his ways are not our ways (Isaiah 55:8).

Much has been written about the theology of suffering and why God does not always answer prayers the way we want. For those wanting an easy-to-read book on this topic, I recommend *God on Mute* by Pete Greig[94] or *The Uninvited Companion* by Scott Shaum.[95] For a more detailed study, try Timothy Keller's *Walking with God through Pain and Suffering*.[96]

Challenging unhelpful thoughts

We can all have negative thoughts about ourselves, others, the world or the future. Accepting and magnifying such thoughts can bring us down and weaken our resilience. Challenging these thoughts by looking for evidence and considering other options can help us to move forward.

For example, someone might think, 'I made a fool of myself today.' It can be helpful to consider both 'Is that true?' and 'Does it matter?' A constructive response is to remind ourselves of biblical truths about God's love for us, and to try to put things in perspective – we all make mistakes. We should dismiss unhelpful expectations, comparisons and pressures, and focus on how God wants us to act in the present moment. We also have a choice about how we deal with unhelpful thoughts about other people. We can choose to complain or to forgive and make the best of the situation.

People who have ongoing patterns of negative thinking may benefit from talking therapy, such as cognitive behavioural therapy.

Choosing to focus on biblical truths

Focusing on Bible passages can enable us to keep God's perspective in mind rather than our own. It can be helpful to memorise verses that strengthen us, and then repeat them in difficult times. We are told, 'Set your minds on things above, not on earthly things' (Colossians 3:2). The apostle Paul wrote:

> Whatever is true, whatever is noble, whatever is right, whatever is pure, whatever is lovely, whatever is admirable – if anything is excellent or praiseworthy – think about such things.
> PHILIPPIANS 4:8

Doing this can help transform and renew our mind (Romans 12:2). When our thinking is in keeping with God's ways, then we will feel more at peace and make wiser choices, and therefore be more resilient.

Creativity

The C in our SPECS model stands not only for cognitive processes, but also for creativity. Being creative in our thoughts and actions is an aspect of resilience that is often overlooked.

We know that God is the creator, and he has made creative people. Adult colouring books are one option for releasing creativity and helping us to relax. There are versions available that centre on Bible verses we can meditate on as we colour. Stories are another example of creativity. Both adults and children can learn a lot through stories, as Jesus realised. Jesus was creative in the parables he told. As his earthly father was a carpenter, Jesus probably also grew up being creative in other ways, using his hands to make things.

Some people enjoy getting lost in a good book or film or in a creative hobby: doodling, drawing, painting, sculpture, craftwork, clay, plasticine, photography, writing, poetry, dance, drama, singing, music, playing, baking, cooking, gardening, sewing, knitting or one of many other creative options. Humour is also creative, showing life in a new perspective. These activities can be good in themselves, purely as enjoyable hobbies or distractions, as described in chapter 6. They can also help release emotions creatively.

Repetitive visuospatial tasks, such as cross-stitch, might help to reduce signs of trauma when performed soon after a traumatic event, which is an additional benefit to the creativity. For those who can't imagine themselves doing cross-stitch, playing video games soon after trauma also seems to reduce traumatic stress symptoms.[97]

Imagination

Mooli Lahad included imagination in his model of resilience, and his work influenced our inclusion of creativity in our model.[98] Lahad described people who cope with stress by daydreaming or imagining pleasant thoughts. Daydreaming about a holiday or a special event can help us feel better, even if it never happens.

The film *Life is Beautiful* presents a moving story about a father who helped his son cope with being in a concentration camp by pretending that it was all a big game. I have come across real-life examples of people using a similar strategy, albeit on a much smaller scale, such as missionary parents who treated an evacuation as a big adventure so that their children were not upset by it. On a trivial level, parents use imagination all the time, for example pretending a spoonful of mush is an aeroplane to persuade their toddler to open their mouth and eat. Imagination can be a powerful tool.

Anne Frank and her Jewish family were forced into hiding from the Nazis. Between the ages of 13 and 15, Anne was confined to an attic, forced to live as a prisoner with no freedom and always with the knowledge that they would be in great danger if they were found. In the end, she died in a concentration camp. Anne wrote in her diary on 3 May 1944:

> I look upon our life in hiding as an interesting adventure, full of danger and romance, and every privation as an amusing addition to my diary… What I'm experiencing here is a good beginning to an interesting life, and that's the reason – the only reason – why I have to laugh at the humorous side of the most dangerous moments.
>
> I'm young and have many hidden qualities; I'm young and strong and living through a big adventure; I'm right in the middle of it and can't spend all day complaining because it's impossible to have any fun! I'm blessed with many things: happiness, a cheerful disposition and strength… Every day I think what a fascinating and amusing adventure this is! With all that, why should I despair?[99]

J.K. Rowling, author of the Harry Potter books, said:

> We do not need magic to transform our world; we carry all the power we need inside ourselves already: we have the power to imagine better.[100]

I heard about one missionary whose favourite way to relax was to go to the beach. As she was serving in a country with no beaches, she missed this opportunity to be refreshed. She decided to take a bowl of warm water, put her feet in it and shut her eyes, pretending she was on the beach. This helped her feel relaxed and happy.

Not everyone likes the feel of sand underneath them. Another missionary, Sue Eenigenburg, writes:

> When we lived in the Middle East, I used to take the kids to play in the park. After bringing the kids home, their shoes would be filled with sand.

Somehow, the kids always seemed to find themselves on my bed, either playing or taking a short nap. The sand would leap willingly from their shoes to slip under the comforter and on to the sheets.

Going to bed at night, my husband would complain about the sand in our sheets. Seeking to avoid having to wash even more laundry, I asked him to imagine that he was having fun sleeping on the beach.[101]

The same author continues:

There is almost always more than one way to look at things that happen in our lives. Seeking to be creative in response to events that take us by surprise is an art that can be developed. I'm not simply lost, I am adventurously trying a new route and enjoying the scenery along the way. Try looking at dust on a coffee table as an opportunity for children to try some finger painting and practice writing skills. Dirty windows ensure that kids will see them and won't try to run through them, thus breaking the glass and injuring themselves.

Creative thinking can even make boring tasks more fun. It can enable us to see the brighter side of dismal events.[102]

In *The Message*, Galatians 6:1–5 refers to creativity twice:

Live creatively, friends. If someone falls into sin, forgivingly restore him, saving your critical comments for yourself. *You* might be needing forgiveness before the day's out... Don't compare yourself with others. Each of you must take responsibility for doing the creative best you can with your own life.

Creative techniques in therapy and spiritual direction

Creative techniques are sometimes used in therapy to help children and adults overcome trauma and other difficulties.[103] Some therapies are obviously creative, such as art, play, poetry, dance or drama therapy. Other therapies may be more traditional but use imagery or creativity at certain points. For example, they might include imagining being in a safe and pleasant place (as a response to anxious feelings), imagining a happier ending to a nightmare or mentally rewinding a flashback.

The imagination is also sometimes used during spiritual direction, perhaps by putting oneself into Bible stories, seeing Jesus in a situation or discussing what we can learn from our dreams.[104]

Building resilience in children: cognitive strategies and creativity

The best way to develop effective cognitive strategies for resilience is to start early. Webster-Stratton has produced excellent, fun little books to help teach young children to problem-solve.[105] Problem-solving is a skill, and like other skills we improve with practice. Teaching others is a good way to improve our own skills in this area, so I encourage people to try teaching these skills to children. We can also teach children to challenge untrue negative thoughts that they might have about themselves or others.

Timmins has written a book about developing resilience in young people,[106] which covers cognitive strategies, such as having a plan B (flexibility), positive thinking (realistic optimism), positive self-talk and reflecting on past successes. Although the book is aimed at young people with autism, the principles can also help young people more widely.

It is important to encourage children to think for themselves, not just to give the 'right' answers. Playing, creativity, imagination and original thoughts should be encouraged. Messy Church is one way to help develop children's creativity in relation to their faith, and there are others.[107]

When teaching Bible stories, instead of just focusing on the facts we can use 'I wonder' questions, such as, 'I wonder which part of the story is the most important?' and 'I wonder which part of the story is most about you?' This has been developed as part of an approach known as Godly Play.[108] Rather than avoiding difficult questions, such as why God does not always do what we ask him to, we can help children to think about such matters in a way appropriate to their level of maturity. We can learn a lot from children when we listen to them.

Linking back to spiritual factors: asking God for wisdom, discernment and inspiration

Human cognitive processes and creativity can only get us so far. God's wisdom, discernment and gentle nudging can get us much further, and we can pray for these gifts.

Trust God from the bottom of your heart;
    don't try to figure out everything on your own.
Listen for God's voice in everything you do, everywhere you go;
    he's the one who will keep you on track.
PROVERBS 3:5–6 (MSG)

In the next chapter, we will consider Joseph, whose cognitive processes included creative prophetic dreams and the ability to interpret the dreams of others. Hearing from God and seeing how God brought good out of suffering were key.

Questions

1 Do you tend to try to find solutions to problems, or do you tend to give up and see the negatives?

2 What do you do when you have unhelpful thoughts?

3 How can we help people, including children, to become better at problem-solving?

4 In what ways are you creative? Is there anything you would like to try to expand your creativity?

5 What do you do to increase your learning?

6 What has been your experience of memorising Bible verses?

9

Resilience in the life of Joseph

One of the key factors in building a resilient life is to find a way of making sense of what happens to us, especially during the difficult times we all go through. If we have a way of interpreting suffering and hardship in a positive light, it will help us persevere when the going is tough.

Joseph's story, told in Genesis 37—50, is one of great hardship and unjust suffering, but one in which he came to find meaning in such a way that he was able not only to endure his difficulties but also to discover God's purpose in them.

Painful days

Joseph, 17 years old, was the favoured son of his father Jacob, and prone to telling tales about his brothers to further ingratiate himself. His father's gift of an ornamented robe for Joseph fuelled the sense of injustice already at work within the brothers, so that they hated him even more and could not say a kind word to him (Genesis 37:1-4).

Joseph had a dream in which his brothers were binding sheaves of corn together. Suddenly, Joseph's sheaf rose up and the other sheaves bowed down to it. The brothers interpreted this as meaning that Joseph thought he was better than them and wanted to rule over them, so their hostility intensified (37:5-7). A second dream, in which the sun, moon and eleven stars were bowing down to Joseph, further enraged them and even brought his father's rebuke (37:9-11).

The brothers felt such animosity towards Joseph that they plotted to kill him, but in the end decided to teach him a lesson by throwing him down a well, before eventually selling him as a slave to some passing Midianite traders. They put blood on his robe and let their father believe that Joseph had been killed by wild animals (37:12-35). Thus Joseph, still a young man, was forcefully separated from his family and his homeland against his will.

Taken to Egypt

The Midianites took Joseph with them to Egypt and sold him to Potiphar, one of Pharaoh's officials. God was with Joseph and he became a trusted servant in Potiphar's house (39:1-6). One day, however, Potiphar's wife made advances towards Joseph. When he refused to sleep with her, she accused him of sexual harassment and he was thrown in prison (39:6-20).

Even in prison God was with Joseph and he gained the favour of the warden (39:20-23). Two of his fellow inmates were the baker and the cupbearer to Pharaoh. Both had dreams that Joseph interpreted for them. On their release the chief baker was executed, but the cupbearer was restored to his position, just as Joseph had foretold. However, the cupbearer forgot all about Joseph's help, and Joseph was left to languish in prison for another two years (40:1-23).

When Pharaoh himself had a series of dreams, the cupbearer encouraged him to seek Joseph's help. God enabled Joseph to interpret the dreams, revealing that there would be seven good years in Egypt followed by seven years of famine. He also suggested that Pharaoh should appoint a wise man to guide the country through this period by storing up grain that could be used when the famine came. The plan pleased Pharaoh and he appointed Joseph to this important position, making him second only to himself in authority. Amazingly, at the age of just 30, Joseph found himself in charge of the whole land of Egypt! He married and had two children during the time of abundance. Then, when famine arrived, he put his plan into operation to successfully save the nation (41:1–57).

Raised up for a purpose

The famine was severe throughout the known world, and back in Israel Jacob's family were suffering. Jacob decided to send his sons down to Egypt to buy grain, and they found themselves bowing down before the governor, asking for his help. The governor, of course, was Joseph, whom they did not recognise, but Joseph realised who they were. Without revealing himself, Joseph set the brothers a series of tests to determine their sincerity (42—44). Eventually Joseph could contain himself no longer, and he made himself known to them (45:1–3).

It is at this point that we are able to see how Joseph sustained himself during the long and painful years of exile. His faith in God had never wavered, despite his sufferings, and he was aware that his success was given by God. His adversity had matured him. Now the complete picture comes into view: 'God sent me ahead of you,' he says to his brothers, 'to preserve for you a remnant on earth and to save your lives by a great deliverance. So then, it was not you who sent me here, but God' (45:7–8). We see now how he is able to find meaning in his suffering and how he interprets the events of his life: God was at work in both his humiliation and his exaltation to bring the divine purposes to pass.

A family reunited

There followed a period of reconciliation with his brothers, and then a reuniting with his father and the wider family who came down to Egypt to join Joseph, 70 people altogether (45:9—46:30). With Pharaoh's permission the sizeable group of Hebrews settled in Goshen and were provided with all the food they needed (46:31—47:12). Some 17 years later, Jacob, now an elderly man, was able to bless his sons and grandsons before he died and was taken back to be buried in Canaan (47:27—50:14).

Joseph and his brothers returned to Egypt, where, in response to their request for his forgiveness, Joseph again explained his understanding of their story as an expression of God's providence: 'You intended to harm me, but God intended it for good to accomplish what is now being done, the saving of many lives. So then, don't be afraid. I will provide for you and your children' (50:20—21). Evil was turned to good, and God's purpose was worked out even through the sinful actions of those involved.

Understanding providence

This belief in the providence of God, so beautifully illustrated throughout the story of Joseph and his brothers, is one that has strengthened God's people in their difficulties ever since the events took place. Providence is the belief that God is guiding human affairs, both good and bad, to bring about his ultimate good purposes. We may not always understand what he is doing at the time, but eventually we can often see how God has shaped things for our good. Providence is best seen with hindsight and requires the eye of faith - it is a way of interpreting the events of our lives, the ups and the downs.

The apostle Paul articulates this conviction most clearly in Romans 8:28: 'And we know that in all things God works for the good of those who love him, who have been called according to his purpose.' It is worth highlighting several truths contained in these words:

- It is God who brings good out of our circumstances. It is not the circumstances themselves that are good; they may well not be good. It requires the action of God to bring good out of evil, as in the case of Joseph.
- No circumstance is outside of God's control – 'all things' means all things.
- While God's providence can be seen in the world in a general way, it is especially noticed in the lives of those who love God and in whom his purpose – to become like Christ – is being worked out (Romans 8:29).
- This does not mean that God is the author of evil. Not everything that happens to us is caused by God, but everything that happens to us is under his control and, in the end, will serve his purpose for us. We make a distinction between God's *directive* will (what he causes to happen) and his *permissive* will (what he allows to happen in respecting human freedom). We live in a fallen world where natural disasters occur and affect us all; sinful human beings hurt one another; we make bad choices ourselves; and Satan is responsible for a lot of the world's evil. Yet God remains in control and, despite all the mess and interference with his plans, can still bring good to pass and accomplish his purposes.

Reflecting on Romans 8:28, pastor Alistair Begg says:

> This great verse is a promise from God that we are not the hapless victims of life, at the mercy of chance or fate. We are not driven by some blind, impersonal force. On the contrary, we are the objects of God's providential care. We are under his guiding and protecting hand.[109]

Eric Liddell, the famous Olympic athlete and missionary to China, who died during Japanese internment in 1945, wrote:

Circumstances may appear to wreck our lives and God's plans, but God is not helpless among the ruins. God's love is still working. He comes in and takes the calamity and uses it victoriously, working out his wonderful plan of love.[110]

These are the assurances we can have when we understand the providence of God and see our lives from God's perspective.

Healing for his pain

The belief in God's guiding hand helped Joseph in his thinking about what had been done to him. Here the spiritual and the cognitive dimensions overlap. It did not, however, make his suffering any the less. Joseph did not deny or minimise the reality of what had happened to him, but he did not let it define him either. He refused to wallow in self-pity. In prison he stated simply, 'I was forcibly carried off from the land of the Hebrews, and even here I have done nothing to deserve being put in a dungeon' (40:15). Family betrayal, physical violence, separation from his loved ones and his familiar culture, followed by gross injustice, cannot have been easy to bear.

No doubt Joseph's healing came about gradually. Time does bring its own healing, and as he gradually began to 'trace the rainbow through the rain'[111] and recognise God's overruling in the events of his life, his pain began to subside. It must have been further helped by his marriage to Asenath and the joy of companionship after his years of loneliness (Genesis 41:45). How good it is to have a soul friend with whom to share one's deepest fears and hurts.

The birth of his two sons took the healing work even further. We know this because of Joseph's own testimony: he called his firstborn Manasseh (which sounds like 'forget' in Hebrew), saying, 'It is because God has made me forget all my trouble and all my father's household' (41:51), and his second son Ephraim (sounding like the Hebrew 'twice fruitful'), saying, 'It is because God has made me fruitful in the land of my suffering' (41:52). Notice that he attributes his healing to God's action in his life. Certainly, having children is a great joy in itself, and the need to step outside of one's own self-absorption to care for others is one of the great growth points that parenthood offers to us; yet Joseph does not fail to recognise the healing grace of God that was at work in his life.

Forgiveness and release

Only when Joseph was reconciled to his brothers was the healing process finally completed. Even then it came in stages, and with great emotional turmoil. On seven occasions we are told of Joseph's tears as his emotions are released, not in polite sobs but in gut-wrenching howls of pain and grief (42:24; 43:30; 45:2, 14–15; 46:29; 50:1, 17). We have seen already how important it is to acknowledge and own our emotions and not to deny or suppress them. We have noted too the healing power of tears. To cry is not a sign of weakness but of strength. Men in particular need to recognise this and forget the idea that 'crying is for wimps'. Joseph found healing because he was willing to be vulnerable, express his feelings and accept his own humanity.

Joseph offered his forgiveness to his brothers when he saw they were truly sorry for their actions (50:16–21). There was no gloating when they threw themselves down before him, no reminding them of his dream. To forgive is an act of the will, not an emotion. It is to release others from the wrong that has been done towards us and is never an easy response to make. However, it is always better that we are able to forgive than to burn up inside with bitterness and hatred. It may take time to come to the place where we are able to do so, but if we refuse to forgive, in the long run we will only harm ourselves and hinder the process of our own recovery and healing.

Happily, Joseph was able to take a further step and be reconciled to his brothers. This is normally a desirable outcome, but it is not always possible and not always the best thing. If there has been abuse or a breakdown of trust, for example, it may not be possible or appropriate to normalise the relationship again. Likewise, if there is no sorrow or humility or acknowledgement of wrongdoing, we may be able to forgive but not restore the relationship. What is important is to guard one's heart from negative emotions that will rob us of our peace and joy, limiting our future growth and effectiveness. Resilient people do their best to work through these issues, often with the help of a third party – a counsellor, spiritual director or mediator. They refuse to get trapped in an ongoing self-destructive bond to a painful past.

Jill Saward was attacked as a young woman when masked men broke into the London vicarage where she lived, tied up and beat her father and boyfriend, and then raped her. She showed great resilience in recovering from her ordeal, and by sharing openly about her trauma she became a champion for the better treatment of women who had suffered sexual violence. At the heart of her recovery was the brave decision to forgive the perpetrators of this horrendous crime. Speaking on TV at the time she said, 'They'd destroyed enough. I didn't want them to destroy anything else. Forgiveness gave me that liberation, that freedom, to move on.'

Wider perspective

It is often said that scripture is the best commentary on scripture. We gain further insight into Joseph's life, and the theology of suffering, from some insights given us by the psalmist:

> He called down famine on the land
>   and destroyed all their supplies of food;
> and he sent a man before them –
>   Joseph, sold as a slave.
> They bruised his feet with shackles,
>   his neck was put in irons,

> till what he foretold came to pass,
>> till the word of the Lord *proved him true*.
>
> PSALM 105:16–19 (my italics)

Here we see what was happening inside Joseph during his sufferings – he was waiting for the fulfilment of his dream but also demonstrating his own faithfulness to God. He was being tested as to his character.

One thing we are told in scripture is that suffering *produces* something in us; if we allow it to shape us, it will have a beneficial effect upon us, refining and purifying us. Thus, Paul writes: 'We also glory in our sufferings, because we know that suffering produces perseverance; perseverance, character; and character, hope' (Romans 5:3–4). The first benefit that can come out of periods of difficulty is that we learn to persevere, not to give up but to keep going. This is a great biblical quality, and the Greek word used here for 'perseverance' (*hupomone*) is the nearest equivalent we have to the modern word 'resilience'. Resilience is formed in us as we face adversity and learn to overcome our challenges. Just as in the gym our muscles are built up as we exercise them, so resilience develops as we learn to endure. This is how character is formed within us, and how we learn to hope in God, for at such times we know we need help from outside ourselves and must depend on him for strength.

Through his trials, Joseph was being prepared for the important role God had for him to play in the future safety of the people of God. He could never have responded so graciously to his brothers had God not first done such a deep work in his own heart. He could not have exercised the power and authority he was given so wisely had he not already been chastened and humbled and made dependent upon God. The higher the calling, the greater the preparation needed. That was true for Joseph, and it will be true for us as well.

Part of Tony's story

My wife and I were missionaries for a number of years in Malaysia, and we loved being there. It was exciting to see God at work, and I loved the adventure of living on the island of Borneo. We expected to be involved in mission for our whole lives, but sadly it did not work out like that. After two terms of service, we were not welcomed back by our mission agency. It was a great blow to us as we were left with a young family and no job, and we were confused as to why this had happened. When the news broke at our church in the UK that we were not returning to Malaysia, the whole congregation burst into applause (they wanted us to stay); I burst into tears for I felt the most precious thing in the world had been taken from me. It took me two years to work through these issues and to transition to life in Britain again, working as a local church pastor. It was only after ten years that I began to understand something of the bigger purpose that had been at work in my life. By this time, I was involved in a missions training programme and pioneering re-entry seminars for those returning from overseas ministry. I found that, because of my own experience of transition, I could help others as they returned, and, because of my own pain, I could understand those who also came back hurting, of whom there were many. God had taken the broken pieces of my life and made something beautiful out of them. He had formed something in me through my disappointment that made me ready for a greater calling on my life.

Questions

1 What do we learn about providence from the story of Joseph? As you look back on your life so far, can you see where providence has been at work, both in your successes and in your difficulties?

2 How did Joseph find healing for his pain? How might you find healing for any pain in your life?

3 Joseph chose to forgive. Is there anyone you have not forgiven? Will you choose to forgive them?

4 Joseph said, 'God has made me forget all my trouble' (Genesis 41:51). We might not literally forget our troubles, but we can choose not to focus on them and not to let them define us. Is there anything in your past that you should choose to stop focusing on and let go of?

5 Think about Romans 5:3–4. Have you ever seen good come out of suffering or difficulties in your own life? What has been produced in your times of adversity?

10

Social and systemic aspects of resilience

Resilience is not just about what happens within a person. Resilience is influenced by what happens between people. 'Social' refers to emotional and practical support from people such as friends, family members and colleagues. 'Systemic' refers to the systems that we are in, including teams and communities. Our environment also influences our resilience, either as a protective factor or as a risk factor.

Family, friends, colleagues and mentors

A large body of research demonstrates that support from people such as friends, family members and colleagues reduces the risk of developing mental health problems, including depression and post-traumatic stress disorder.[112] People who feel socially isolated are at higher risk of mental health difficulties. Giving support, as well as receiving support, can be good for us. However, those who give out a lot to others need to be especially careful that they have enough people who enrich their lives and care for them, otherwise they may become drained.

Wilson and Wilson write, 'Joy comes from other people... You may need to think carefully about which people increase your happiness in God, and seek them out. You probably already know who they are: people who, when you've finished being with them, make you more joyful in who God is and what he's done. Ring them. Get time with them. And pass the effect on to others.'[113]

Social support can include support from a mentor, spiritual director or another helper. Proverbs 27:17 states, 'As iron sharpens iron, so one person sharpens another.' It has been said that we all need a Paul to mentor us, a Barnabas to encourage us and a Timothy we can mentor (who may be a child). This reminds us that there are different types of relationships we can benefit from.

It takes time to nurture healthy relationships – whether with a spouse, family members, friends or colleagues. Without time, we cannot build relationships. Other ingredients of good, supportive relationships include love, forgiveness and listening skills. With those basics in place, we can go a long way.

Marriage

For people who are married, their spouse should generally be a major source of support (although if they are very unwell they may not be able to function in this role and other support will be needed). Crawford and Carr conducted research with missionaries.[114] One part of their investigation involved studying whether the strength of a marriage relationship helped to predict the resilience of the couple. In response, one husband reported, 'Marital status does not impact resilience as much as with whom I am married. In other words, my wife is a huge factor in resilience for *me*.'[115] Another person added that the effect of marital status on resilience was:

Negative or positive depending on the season of our marriage. Unresolved conflict/struggles can bring extra stress...

However, when our marriage is working well, it strengthens my resilience.[116]

A third person said that her marital status had no effect on her resilience. She explained:

In fact, the extra toll of caring for a family takes time away from my being able to spend ample time in the word and in prayer or with a friend... For me, resilience isn't in having a husband. It is in dwelling in the place (God's presence) that gives you the strength of resilience you need.[117]

These quotations are fairly typical, and illustrate that marriage may boost or weaken resilience, depending on the strength of the relationship and the time available for maintaining a walk with God. Children can bring tremendous joy, but difficulties with children (or other family members) can be a particular source of stress and sadness, leaving less energy for responding to other challenges.

Marriages take time and effort, and a willingness to consider the needs of the other person. Gary Thomas suggests that we should think about the purpose of marriage as being not for our happiness but for our holiness.[118] That can change our attitude and create a more resilient marriage.

Singleness

Single people may also benefit from thinking about holiness being the goal, rather than happiness. The study mentioned above found that resilience has more to do with the individual and the quality of their relationships than with whether or not they are married. Being single does not mean that someone is less resilient than their married peers, but it is important for single people to put time into building strong relationships, as well as into their spiritual life.

Most people want to have at least one deep relationship with someone they can confide in, who gives them attention and support. People who do not have such a confidant can feel very isolated. Ideally, we want more than just one confidant; we want to feel part of a caring community. People who struggle with their singleness or childlessness may find it helpful to receive counselling or spiritual direction, as an extra supportive and helping relationship.

Systemic and environmental aspects of resilience

In earlier chapters, we discussed the importance of spiritual care, which is central to resilience. We have also discussed self-care through looking after ourselves physically, emotionally and in our thought life. We have just considered the importance of caring for one another, as family members and friends.[119]

Next, we are going to consider systemic factors – the systems around us, such as teams, communities, churches, organisations, government and wider society. We will also discuss more general environmental factors, such as security, culture and living conditions, which are influenced by the systems we live in.

Systemic challenges do not necessarily make us less resilient. For example, Jesus endured opposition and hostility, and he did not have his own home, yet he was the most resilient person I can think of. Systemic and environmental challenges can increase our resilience if we become stronger through coping with the difficulties. However, a demanding environment can take a lot of our energy. If we do not have sufficient resources to cope with the challenges, we start to suffer from stress or anxiety.

Our model of resilience is illustrated in the diagram on the next page. The personal aspects of resilience (contained within an individual) are shown as petals on a flower. The social and systemic aspects are shown as the soil (or conditions) in which the flower grows. These may help it to flourish, or they may cause problems. Just as a plant needs nutrients, water, light and air to be healthy, so humans need certain conditions around them in order to thrive. We have already discussed support from family, friends, colleagues and mentors. Next we will discuss more systemic and environmental factors. I am not attempting to list every systemic aspect imaginable, but just to discuss some of the important ones.

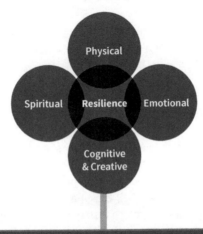

Social and Systemic			
Family	Friends	Colleagues	Mentors
Security	Finance & Work	Climate	Government & Policies
Living Conditions	Culture	Church/ Organisation	Team & Community

Security

It is easier to be resilient if we feel that we are living in a relatively secure location. If we live in an insecure context, such as a war zone, a lot of our energy may be taken up monitoring and evaluating our situation. Daily life can take a lot of effort, and the stress may have a physical impact on us (for example, causing sleeping problems). Good security awareness and training can reduce our anxiety and enhance resilience in an insecure environment.

Security can be at a personal level as well as at a wider level. People who feel personally under attack or harassed may find their resilience reserves being depleted.

Finance and work

People who have financial reserves may seem more resilient in the face of difficulties, such as health problems or the loss of a job, as they know that they will be able to cope financially. Those who are already struggling to pay their bills may feel less able to cope with such difficulties and therefore less resilient. Having said this, we should not underestimate the inner resilience of those who manage to go on despite their poverty. Finance is only one part of the 'soil' and, although it has an impact, many people have remarkable inner resources of resilience despite living in poverty.

When work is going well, people tend to feel happier and more fulfilled. When work is unenjoyable or going badly, or involves a role that is not a good fit, people often feel miserable. Those who are employed full-time spend many hours at work, and so it is not surprising that work has an impact on well-being. Having to work overly long hours may lead to poorer quality of life. Those who are unemployed may find that this reduces their self-esteem, as well as having financial implications.

Climate

Extreme heat may cause fatigue and make us less productive than we would be in a cooler climate. Extreme coldness can also slow us down. A lack of sunlight may lower mood. Drought has an impact on the availability of food. Different people prefer different climates for their optimal resilience level.

Government and policies

Government and social policies affect all areas of life, from the freedom to share our faith or our right to work (or even to remain in a country) to provision for welfare or education. Health systems are also affected by government policy and can have a significant impact on life.

Living conditions

Having a home where we feel settled, and expecting that we will be able to remain in that home, can add to our resilience. Feeling unsettled or unhappy with our living conditions can be very draining. Unsafe living conditions, including a lack of hygiene, can be a physical risk. Coping with homelessness can take all our physical, mental and emotional energy and leave little capacity for other aspects of life.

Culture

Cultural attitudes and coping mechanisms are likely to have an impact on resilience. The poem 'If' by Rudyard Kipling opens with the following words:

If you can keep your head when all about you
    Are losing theirs and blaming it on you,

If you can trust yourself when all men doubt you,
    But make allowance for their doubting too;
If you can wait and not be tired by waiting,
    Or being lied about, don't deal in lies…

The poem ends with assurance that if you can do all this, 'you'll be a Man, my son!'

This is a typically British picture of resilience (right down to waiting in queues). Such behaviour might be interpreted by people from some cultures as an unhealthy denial of emotions. Different cultures have different expectations of how (or whether) emotions should be expressed, and coping strategies differ from culture to culture. In some cultures, it is normal for those who are bereaved to wail loudly, while other cultures discourage crying. Bereavement rituals may help in coping longer-term.[120] In some cultures shouting and arguing are viewed as normal, whereas in other places shouting is unacceptable. In general, a resilient person will feel able to tolerate their emotions and to express them in ways that they themselves (and most others in their culture) feel is reasonable and not an overreaction. However, sometimes it may be a sign of resilience to be able to go against cultural norms – for example, by crying despite a cultural view that crying is a sign of weakness. Cultures that encourage some expression of emotion may be better at enhancing resilience.

In resource-rich cultures, there is often an expectation that life will be comfortable, which means that when we face difficulties we protest and feel low or angry because this is not what we expected. In resource-poor nations, there is more often an expectation that life will be hard. Consequently, there is more acceptance of difficulties, and often considerable resilience in meeting the challenges of daily life. Communal cultures generally have better models of support than individualistic cultures.

Research has found that mental illness is three times as common in 'rich countries with bigger rather than smaller income differences between rich and poor' than in countries where there is not such a large gap between the wealthy and the poor, and this difference is apparently 'not a matter of awareness, definitions or treatment'.[121] It is clear that there are cultural differences in resilience, but we do not yet fully understand how these differences operate.

People who live outside their own culture may feel that their resilience is reduced, as it can be tiring to work out cultural cues and to function in a different language. However, some people thrive in a new culture if they enjoy their new lifestyle.

Church (and mission organisations)

A church should be an example of community working at its best, with care and support for all. There should be opportunities to pray together and to grow in faith, for example by meeting in small groups.

Churches and organisations that send workers to new cultures have a duty of care to meet certain requirements. These include appropriate recruitment and placement; risk assessment and contingency planning; preparation; and support while the worker is away and also at the end of the period of service. When a family travels together the care should be for the whole family. A mission lifestyle can involve frequently uprooting from the 'soil' we are in, with lots of coming and going. This can be difficult, and things can feel chaotic, so the sending church or mission organisation needs to provide support and stability.

Team and community

Many people are in a team in some aspect of their life, whether at work, for the church, in a ministry team or in a group they belong to. Teams that function well and are supportive help build resilience. People who cooperate with each other and assist one another can form a more resilient team than individuals who function at a high level but in isolation. It is the overall mix that is important in creating a resilient team. As Barrett and Martin put it:

> Agreeable and sociable extraverts may be part of the social glue that binds the team together, but the conscientious and detail-focused planners are needed to ensure that the tasks are completed... Bad moods can be infectious: one neurotic individual can bring down a whole team... Team members must also trust each other, as well as being trustworthy and reliable themselves.[122]

Dysfunctional teams sap motivation and energy, causing stress and dissatisfaction. In multicultural teams, people may struggle to understand why those from different cultures do things in a different way. Taking time to listen to each team member and to try to see things from their perspective is worthwhile.

Delegation is a useful skill in a team – for example, being able to cover while one person goes on holiday or is sick, or if someone feels overloaded or is unable to focus on their primary task (see, for example, Acts 6:1–4).

We may also be part of a community that differs from the team we work in. The community can include neighbours, shopkeepers and others who provide services. Where there is a strong sense of community, people look out for one another, and help and value one another. This builds resilience. We can nurture a sense of community through acts of kindness and showing care to those around us, and especially those in need. Trying to be a brave role model for others can help reduce our own fears as well as the fears of other people.[123] Being part of a courageous community can make us more courageous and resilient than we would be alone.

Good leadership helps to build resilient teams, while poor leadership weakens a team. Teams desire authentic leaders who practise what they preach, and lead by their actions not just with words. Authentic leaders have been defined as leaders who openly share information and feelings; objectively analyse data before making a decision; are guided by internal moral standards; and are self-aware (knowing their own strengths and weaknesses).[124] Trust in the leadership influences how team members feel and behave.

Building resilience in children: social and systemic aspects

Caregivers (usually the parents) and siblings are generally the most important people in the lives of young children. As they grow older, friends become increasingly important. As well as helping children to feel loved and giving them attention, caregivers should give them opportunities to make friends by letting them spend time with other children. Some children need guidance on how to make and maintain friendships, but many children just need opportunities. School, clubs and play dates can all help.

When considering moving to a new area, it is important to consider what the impact will be on the children. Moving during the adolescent years, when the child is already dealing with issues related to identity and when friendships are very important, can be especially difficult. Time should be taken to prepare and support children through the transition.

Social media can be an important way for children and teenagers to connect with their friends. However, social media also has the potential to harm. This can be through spending too much time online to the detriment of other areas of life; bullying; feeling inadequate due to comparisons with others or not getting enough 'likes'; or more sinister activities, such as sexting, grooming or viewing pornography. Children need guidance and support in making the most of social media while minimising the risks.[125]

Linking back to spiritual factors: Christian lifestyles

Christians aim to live as a community of the people of God. If we demonstrate love, patience, mercy and forgiveness, as taught in the Bible, we have a good chance of building positive relationships.

When considering Christian leaders, character is important, not just skill. The *Growing Leaders*[126] book and course focus on character development for leaders, aiming for the development of godly wisdom and Christlikeness. In the next chapter, we will consider how Jesus, the model authentic leader, built up resilience in his community of disciples.

Questions

1 How well supported are you? What could you do to improve your relationships?

2 How deep are your friendships?

3 Do you have a Paul, a Barnabas and a Timothy in your life?

4 How can you help others, including children, build good relationships?

5 Describe the 'soil' you are living in. Which aspects help you thrive, and which hinder you?

6 Do you consider your church to be 'healthy soil'? Why, or why not?

11

A community of resilient disciples

In his upper room discourse (John 13—17), Jesus begins to prepare his disciples for life without him and for carrying on his work when he has returned to the Father. His teaching, given shortly before his death, is a masterclass in how to build resilience in others.

Jesus had demonstrated resilience by his example, but now his teaching would equip his followers for the loss associated with his departure and the challenges ahead. In the privacy of the upper room, he shared his final instructions with them, highlighting several key ways by which they could strengthen and resource themselves. What he said to them is applicable to all who live as disciples of Christ in a hostile world.

The disciples were a disparate bunch and, though hand-picked by Jesus, did not gel easily. Indeed, they had their moments of strife, disagreement and petty jealousy. Over the three years that they were privileged to be with him, Jesus slowly formed them into a unit, a band of brothers who would be able to continue the work that he had started. Yes, they were often slow to learn the lessons he had to teach them, but Jesus remained confident that they would be able to take the gospel message to the ends of the earth.

That night, Jesus commissioned them to continue the work he began: 'You did not choose me, but I chose you and appointed you so that you might go and bear fruit – fruit that will last' (15:16). The sense of being part of something worthwhile, of having a noble task to perform, aids resilience, as does knowing that someone we look up to believes we can be successful. The disciples must have felt this as they listened to the Master's words. The awareness that we have been called by God to a particular task, and to carry a sense of vocation for it, greatly enhances our ability to persevere when the going is tough.

Be prepared for hardship

Jesus made it clear to his disciples that continuing his work in the world meant they would suffer. The cost of discipleship is not hidden in the small print. If the Master was despised, so will be the servant. He told them plainly, 'If the world hates you, keep in mind that it hated me first… If they persecuted me, they will persecute you also' (15:18, 20). Furthermore, Jesus was specific about some of the hardships they would face. 'They will put you out of the synagogue,' he said, 'in fact, the time is coming when anyone who kills you will think they are offering a service to God' (16:2).

This, of course, is the daily reality for many believers today. According to Open Doors, over 200 million Christians around the world are persecuted because of their faith. They are beaten, killed, forcibly detained and denied education or job opportunities; their churches and homes are bombed and burned, and their children abducted. This is happening in more than 50 countries.[127] At the same time, in many so-called Christian countries there is a growing opposition to Christian values and standards, especially in the public arena.

We should not be surprised by this, even if we are saddened by it and long for something better. Neither should we be frightened by it. Jesus said, 'I have told you these things, so that in me you may have peace. In this world you will have trouble. But take heart! I have overcome the world' (16:33).

Knowing that suffering is a possibility for anyone who takes following Jesus seriously helps us to prepare for the realities we may face. To be forewarned is to be forearmed (16:4). It is better to be realistic about the nature of Christian ministry than to make idealistic assumptions that leave no room for struggle. This is why individual and group resilience is increased when people are well prepared for the challenges ahead, and why having a robust theology of suffering is essential in making sense of unexpected adversity.

Be part of a believing community

From the beginning Jesus had sought to shape his followers into a community. Although he spoke only briefly about the church (Matthew 16:18; 18:17), it seems clear that he had in mind the establishment of a new community of those called to be his followers and committed to living in obedience to his commands. In the last chapter, we saw that resilient people are characterised by establishing good support networks. Jesus anticipated that his followers would automatically provide the kind of mutual support for one another that would strengthen them for their task.

Being in community provides a sense of belonging and of being part of something bigger, which also aids individual resilience. It is far healthier to be part of a team than to work alone. Schaefer and Schaefer comment:

> Human resilience depends on the ability to closely connect with at least a few other people. Openness and vulnerability allow for the kind of depth in relationships that encourages truly facing and moving beyond struggles... Resilient people are more *inter*dependent than *in*dependent. When life hits hard, they entrust themselves to others and accept help and support.[128]

Community gives us a safe place in times of need, a shelter from the storms of life.

Make friendship a priority

In the intimate setting of the upper room, Jesus reminded his disciples that he regarded them as friends, not simply as servants (15:13–15). It is interesting to see that this conversation took place over a meal (13:1–2). Passover was not only a major religious festival; it was also an important social occasion. Friendship thrives on people having time to be together, and the meal table provides a real focus for conversation, sharing and encouragement. When it comes to building enduring and effective relationships, we must be willing to put some effort into getting to know and understand each other. Not only will this reduce friction as we work together, but it will also strengthen the bonds between us so that when we are under pressure we are more likely to hold together and come through the difficulties all the stronger.

Despite being connected with others through social media and the internet, many people find loneliness is still a major issue for them. The absence of at least a few deep and lasting friendships leaves us more vulnerable to depression and discouragement. That is why it is important to seek supportive friendships and to make time to nurture life-giving relationships. It is a mistake to be too busy for friendship or to allow oneself to become socially isolated because of the pressure of work. Scripture wisely says:

> Two are better than one,
>   because they have a good return for their labour:
> if either of them falls down,
>   one can help the other up.
> But pity anyone who falls
>   and has no one to help them up.
> ECCLESIASTES 4:9–10

Be willing to receive help

When the meal was finished, Jesus demonstrated his love for his disciples in a surprising way. He adopted the role of a servant, and, taking off his outer garments, took a towel and a bowl of water and began to wash his disciples' feet. This was first and foremost a simple act of love and a demonstration of the fact that Jesus was the true servant (13:2–5; Isaiah 42:1–3; Mark 10:45; Philippians 2:5–11). It showed how much he valued each of them, and cared for their well-being. It was also an acted parable, for it foreshadowed the cleansing from sin that would be available after the cross.

At first Peter resisted the kindness of Jesus, feeling unworthy of his Master's attention. When he understood that he could not be in relationship with Jesus unless he submitted to this act of love, he then wanted to be washed all over (13:6–9)! Peter's initial response is typical of those in ministry or caring roles who are used to giving out to others but who are less willing to receive help. There is a certain vulnerability in allowing Jesus (or his servants) to minister to us, but all of us occasionally need to receive his gentle, loving touch. There is no need for us to soldier on, continually putting others first and neglecting our own needs in the meantime. This is folly, and it leaves us in danger. Resilient people have the humility to ask for help and to allow others to get close enough to help them. They are not afraid to be vulnerable and can see the danger in being too self-reliant or self-contained.

Wash one another's feet

In demonstrating his own servant heart, Jesus set an example for his disciples to follow. 'Now that I, your Lord and Teacher, have washed your feet,' he said, 'you also should wash one another's feet. I have set you an example that you should do as I have done for you' (13:14–15). The new community that Jesus had in mind is characterised by servanthood. 'Washing one another's feet' represents for us the willingness to serve one another in ordinary, everyday kinds of ways (1 Timothy 5:10). Wallace Benn says, 'The love that Jesus patterns is practical and sacrificial. It is the kind of love that considers the needs of others, and it is willing to meet those needs even when it is costly.'[129] Being part of such a community means that sometimes we will be able to give to others and help them in their time of need; but it also means that they will be there for us in our time of need. This is the essence of supportive community.

Love one another

Not surprisingly, the chief characteristic of the new community is to be love. This is not a sentimental love characterised by warm feelings, but a love like that modelled by Jesus – sacrificial in its expression, accepting in its outlook and broad in its appeal. 'A new command I give you: love one another,' said Jesus. 'As I have loved you, so you must love one another. By this everyone will know that you are my disciples, if you love one another' (13:34–35). For good measure Jesus repeated himself twice more (15:12, 17). It is clear that love is to be the foundation of relationships within the Christian community. All of us, without exception, need to be part of such a group. In order to mature, we need to learn to give love; in order to thrive, we need to learn to receive love.

No church, of course, is perfect. Ministry teams, too, have their challenges, and mission communities their struggles. Christian community is for the imperfect, people-in-progress who are seeking to grow and change but are not yet the finished article. Often, we are disappointed by people, and they are probably disappointed by us. Eugene Peterson testifies honestly, 'Every time I move to a new community, I find a church close by and join it – committing myself to worship and work with that company of God's people. I've never been anything other than disappointed.'[130] Yet, frustrating as it sometimes may be, most of the time it is actually wonderful to be part of a community where we are known and loved for who we are, where we are encouraged in our faith and prayed for in our need. We are strengthened by belonging to a community of faith.

Be willing to trust God

We have seen that faith in God is an essential ingredient in a resilient life. Jesus knew that in the days ahead, when he was no longer with them, his disciples would often feel perplexed and afraid, lonely and full of grief. His return to the Father would leave them bereft. He asked that they trust him as they trusted his Father: 'Do not let your hearts be troubled. You believe in God; believe also in me' (14:1). Trust is faith in a dark place; it is holding on to God and his word when we do not understand what is happening or why. To trust another person completely is the highest compliment we can give them. That is why God is delighted when he sees that his people choose to trust him in the midst of their difficulties and pain.

Brennan Manning says, 'The faith that animates the Christian community is less a matter of believing in the existence of God than a practical trust in his loving care under whatever pressure.'[131] To animate something means to give life to it. That which gives life to our relationship with God is the trust we show as we traverse the ups and downs of our journey with him. Jesus understood this and sought to cultivate that wonderful relationship of trust with his disciples.

He reassured them in three different ways.

- 'You do not realise now what I am doing, but later you will understand' (13:7). Initially we may be confused and bewildered by the ways of God, but after the passing of time, and when we can look with hindsight, we will be able to make sense of it all. It requires trust to take those first steps of faith, without a map, without an assurance of the destination, and to believe that one day we will understand.

- 'I am telling you now before it happens, so that when it does happen you will believe that I am who I am' (13:19). Some of the promises Jesus made were yet to be fulfilled. They were still in the future. He asked that they remember what he had said and trust him for the fulfilment, to hold on to his word until it came to pass. When it happened, their faith would be rewarded, and they would have great assurance.

- 'My Father's house has many rooms; if that were not so, would I have told you that I am going there to prepare a place for you? And if I go and prepare a place for you, I will come back and take you to be with me that you also may be where I am' (14:2–3). When Jesus leaves them to return to his Father, they will feel bereft and alone, but his promise was that he would return. In the meantime, they will have to wait for that day. It requires trust to believe that someone is as good as their word.

The result of trusting God in this way is that, instead of being troubled and afraid, we find his peace begins to take hold of our hearts. This is why Jesus said to them, 'Peace I leave with you; my peace I give you. I do not give to you as the world gives. Do not let your hearts be troubled and do not be afraid' (14:27). Peace in this sense means an inner calmness, a stability of heart and mind, and a quiet assurance that things will work out for the best. This inward peace – a gift from God – provides a good basis for a resilient life.

Be dependent on the Holy Spirit

As disciples, we are not dependent on our own resources. The Holy Spirit has been given to us to equip us and strengthen us for the task. There is more teaching about the Holy Spirit in this section of John's gospel than in any other part of the Bible. The fact that Jesus used his last moments with his disciples before his arrest to teach them about the Holy Spirit shows how important it is that we get to know the Holy Spirit and experience his help in our lives. See, for example, John 14:15–18, 25–27; 15:26–27; 16:7–15. Of course, secular literature makes no mention of this dimension when it looks at the possible sources of resilience, but for Christians this is hugely significant.

The disciples were rightly filled with grief at the thought of being separated from Jesus, but he was at pains to reassure them that it was actually to their benefit that he went away. Why? Because if he did not go away the Holy Spirit would not come to them (16:5–7). Jesus promised them that he would not leave them as orphans, but would come to them, by which he meant in the person of the Holy Spirit (14:18). This was what happened on the day of Pentecost, and it brought about a whole new way of experiencing God: 'But you know him, for he lives *with* you and will be *in* you' (14:17, my italics). Previously the work of the Holy Spirit had been external (with you); after Pentecost it would also be internal (in you). In this way the life of Christ would be available to every believer without limitation, through the indwelling Spirit.

The main task of the Holy Spirit is to equip and empower us for Christian life and ministry, and Jesus made it clear that we should not proceed without knowing his presence in our lives. Speaking about the Spirit, Jesus said to his disciples, 'I am going to send you what my Father has promised; but stay in the city until you have been clothed with power from on high' (Luke 24:49). It is vital that as believers we are filled with the Holy Spirit (Ephesians 5:18), which means to live daily under his control and in dependency upon his power. This is an essential prerequisite for effective Christian life and ministry, and a major strand in our resilience. We cannot afford to neglect the Spirit's work in our lives.

Be deeply connected to Jesus

In speaking to his disciples in the upper room, Jesus made use of a powerful illustration from nature to teach them about the importance of living in a deep relationship with himself. He said, 'I am the vine; you are the branches. If you remain in me and I in

you, you will bear much fruit; apart from me you can do nothing'
(15:5). The point he is making is simple yet profound. The branch
does not have to produce the fruit by itself. Indeed, it cannot. All it
needs to do is to stay connected to the vine, then the life of the vine
will produce the fruit naturally and without effort. What this means
is that effectiveness in Christian ministry is not dependent upon our
own efforts. It is not by the sweat of our brow or by the might of our
labours that we produce results; it is by allowing Christ to work in us
and through us.

One of the pitfalls of Christian ministry is that we think everything
depends upon us. This motivates us to work long and hard, but
without much effect. This in turn is the reason why so many
experience burnout or exhaustion, which decrease their resilience.
Effective service for Christ is only sustainable over the long haul if
we learn to stay connected to Christ and learn to work in partnership
with him. This is why Peter refused to take the credit for the healing
of the crippled beggar in Acts 3. He said, 'Why do you stare at us
as if by our own power or godliness we had made this man walk?'
(v. 12) He knew full well that it was God who was responsible for the
healing, not himself.

What all this underlines for us again is the importance of nurturing
and developing the inner life as a key factor in building our resilience.
To abide in Christ requires that we connect with him through the
disciplines of grace, such as prayer, scripture and worship. It means
we need to take time to be with him and to listen to his voice, and to
cultivate greater inwardness through stillness, silence and solitude.
In particular, we need to cultivate the awareness of our dependency
on God. All this, of course, runs counter to our natural tendency to
be constantly busy and relentlessly active as we try to make things
happen. At first, we will feel awkward and perhaps guilty that we are
not as busy as we feel we ought to be, but gradually we will realise
that sometimes less is more. Abiding in Christ is not doing nothing;
it is doing the one thing that will sustain us in ministry and enhance
our resilience. It has to be a priority for us.

Be aware that Jesus prays for you

The final point from the upper room comes from John 17, where Jesus prays for himself and then for his disciples. It is sometimes called the high priestly prayer of Jesus, and it is a reminder that Jesus is now at the Father's right hand, interceding for his church (Hebrews 4:14–16; 7:25). His heavenly ministry is summed up succinctly in 17:9: 'I pray for them.' This truth is often neglected in Christian teaching, but provides a great encouragement to us in our times of need. A central focus for his prayer comes in 17:11:

> I will remain in the world no longer, but they are still in the world, and I am coming to you. Holy Father, protect them by the power of your name, the name you gave me, so that they may be one as we are one.

How relevant is that for a church operating in a climate of hostility? And then again in 17:15: 'My prayer is not that you take them out of the world but that you protect them from the evil one.'

Secular research will never uncover the significance of this factor in our resilience. Its effectiveness may even be hidden from our own eyes, yet how reassuring it is to know that the risen Lord prays for his people! We know the effectiveness of the prayers of other people on our behalf. How much more effective are the prayers of the Saviour?

Questions

1 Jesus' disciples 'had their moments of strife, disagreement and petty jealousy', but Jesus formed them into 'a band of brothers who would be able to continue the work'. Have you ever been part of a church, team or community that has gone through conflict or disunity and come out stronger? If so, what helped?

2 Are you part of a caring community? If not, how might you find this kind of support?

3 Jesus warned his disciples that they would be persecuted. The systemic factors around us may be hostile, insecure or challenging in other ways. Which aspects in your environment do you find challenging, and what helps you to cope?

4 Do you ever find it difficult to receive help from others? Remember that asking for help is not a sign of weakness.

5 What is your current experience of the Holy Spirit?

12

Resilient women in the Bible

The Bible devotes a lot more pages to male characters than to female ones. This is not surprising given the culture at the time that it was written. Nevertheless, despite cultural expectations, women have important roles in the Bible. These include saving Moses from death (Exodus 1:17—2:10); leading Israel as a prophet and judge (Judges 4:4–9); giving birth to the Saviour of the world (Luke 2:7); prophesying over Jesus in the temple (Luke 2:36–38); providing the financial support for Jesus' ministry (Luke 8:2–3); and being the first to witness Jesus' resurrection (Mark 16:1–6; Luke 24:1–6).

We can find examples of each of the five domains of resilience that we have been looking at among women in the Bible. Some of these women only have a few verses written about them, so we have less to say about them than about the male characters we discuss in this book. Nevertheless, what we do know about these women is significant. In this chapter, we will consider the resilience of five women in difficult circumstances.

Spiritual resilience: Mary

It is thought that Mary was just a teenager when the angel appeared to her and told her that she was going to have a baby – not just any baby, but the Son of God. Carrying the Messiah did not mean that she was going to have an easy ride. Her fiancé, Joseph, nearly broke off their engagement because of the disgrace of Mary's pregnancy (Matthew 1:19), and it took an angel to persuade Joseph to marry Mary. Then the Romans announced a census, so Joseph and his pregnant wife had an uncomfortable journey to Bethlehem. There was no room for them at the inn, so the baby was placed in a manger. The couple were too poor to afford the more costly temple sacrifice of a lamb, so they offered two birds instead (Luke 2:24; see Leviticus 12:7–8).

Scorn, discomfort, pain and poverty were just the start of it. Simeon gave a prophecy to Mary that 'a sword will pierce your own soul' (Luke 2:35). King Herod wanted to kill Jesus, so the family fled by night to Egypt, as homeless refugees (Matthew 2:14). After Herod died, they uprooted once again and moved back to Nazareth (Matthew 2:21–23).

Mary must have been resilient to cope with all this occurring in just a few years. Her resilience was tested to the limits when she stood at the foot of the cross watching her firstborn son die (John 19:25). Jesus asked his disciple John to look after Mary, so we can assume that she was by now a widow (John 19:26–27). Mary did not give up or hide out of fear of what might happen to her. In the book of Acts, after Jesus' death and resurrection, we read that Mary continued to pray constantly with the remaining disciples (Acts 1:14).

Her life of prayer and faith appears to be the key to her resilience. Mary knew that her calling was to raise the Messiah. She accepted this in obedience and trust, saying, 'I am the Lord's servant' (Luke 1:38). When she visited her relative Elizabeth, Mary spoke out a song of praise that echoed the praise of Hannah when she too had a son (see later in this chapter):

> My soul glorifies the Lord
> and my spirit rejoices in God my Saviour…
> holy is his name.

His mercy extends to those who fear him,
from generation to generation...
     he has scattered those who are proud in their inmost
     thoughts.
He has brought down rulers from their thrones
     but has lifted up the humble.
He has filled the hungry with good things
     but has sent the rich away empty.

LUKE 1:46–53

Before Jesus performed his first recorded miracle, at the wedding in Cana, Mary demonstrated hope and confidence that he *could* do a miracle. She told the servants, 'Do whatever he tells you' (John 2:5). When they did, a miracle happened and water was turned into wine.

Mary demonstrates key characteristics of spiritual resilience: a sense of hope, calling and meaning; gratitude and praise; trust; faith; and dependence on God's mercy and forgiveness. She lived in obedience to God, and she prayed. She took time to be still and ponder in her heart, contemplating what God was doing: 'Mary treasured up all these things and pondered them in her heart' (Luke 2:19); 'His mother held these things dearly, deep within herself' (Luke 2:51, MSG).

Perhaps Mary was chosen to give birth to the Messiah because she was especially devoted to God and full of faith. Certainly, her spiritual resilience must have helped her in her darkest times.

Physical resilience: Hagar

We read in Genesis that because Abram had no children by the time he was 85 years old, his wife Sarai told him to sleep with her servant Hagar so that they could have a child. Abram did so, and Hagar became pregnant. Then Sarai grew jealous and ill-treated Hagar.

Hagar had a physical way of responding. She ran away to the desert, stopping near a stream (Genesis 16:6–8). An angel appeared to her there, and asked what she was doing (similar to the way in which an angel later appeared to Elijah in the desert, and God asked Elijah what he was doing). This angel told Hagar to return to her mistress, and promised that God would give Hagar so many descendants that they would be impossible to count (16:9–10).

Hagar returned to Sarai and Abram. Hagar was aware of her physical senses and called God 'the God who sees me' (16:13). She named her son Ishmael, meaning 'God listens'.

Ishmael was circumcised when he was 13 (17:24–25). A year later Sarai (now known as Sarah) had a son, Isaac. When Isaac was weaned, Sarah saw Ishmael mocking, and Sarah told Abram (now Abraham) to get rid of Hagar and Ishmael (21:9–10).

Having heard from God, Abraham gave Hagar food and sent her and Ishmael away. Sometimes resilient people stay during a crisis, and sometimes they go. Hagar left the situation. She walked to the desert, carrying the food and water on her shoulders – showing physical strength at a time of vulnerability. When they ran out of water, Hagar expected her son to die and could not bear to watch. God showed her a well nearby, and she was able to give Ishmael water (21:19). They continued to live in the desert, with Hagar (now a single parent) finding food for them both.

Like thousands of women around the world today, Hagar was used to physical hard work. First, she was a servant, and then when she was a homeless displaced person she must have worked to provide shelter and food for herself and her son. Like many women today, she had been treated badly. She was used for sex. There are only a few Bible verses about Hagar, so we do not know a lot about her.

Hagar was resilient despite having seemingly no support from others. As well as having physical strength, she also heard from God.

With God's help she was able to provide for herself and her son. May this be true also for those in the world today who are exploited and ill-treated.

Emotional resilience: Hannah

We read about Hannah in the book of 1 Samuel. Hannah demonstrates emotion-focused coping. Because she was a barren woman, she was teased by her husband's other wife, Peninnah, who had sons and daughters. When Peninnah taunted her, Hannah cried, which led to her husband comforting her.

Hannah also cried about her childlessness. As well as crying, Hannah prayed fervently, telling God her feelings and desires:

> In her deep anguish Hannah prayed to the Lord, weeping bitterly. And she made a vow, saying, 'Lord Almighty, if you will only look on your servant's misery and remember me, and not forget your servant but give her a son, then I will give him to the Lord for all the days of his life.'
>
> 1 SAMUEL 1:10–11

Hannah continued for so long in silent, fervent prayer that Eli the priest assumed she was drunk, and he scolded her. Hannah told him that she had not been drinking but was 'pouring out [her] soul to the Lord' and praying out of 'great anguish and grief' (1:15–16). Eli blessed her, and Hannah's mood lifted.

God answered Hannah's prayer and she gave birth to a son, Samuel. Hannah was able to rejoice in the birth of her son, even while knowing that after weaning him she would hand him over to be raised in the temple, as a child dedicated to God. She expressed her emotions again when she handed him over to Eli, but this time they were joyful. She prayed:

My heart rejoices in the Lord…
There is no one holy like the Lord…
Those who were full hire themselves out for food,
    but those who were hungry are hungry no more…
he humbles and he exalts.

1 SAMUEL 2:1–2, 5, 7

Or, as it says in *The Message* version:

I'm bursting with God-news!
    I'm walking on air…
    I'm dancing my salvation

1 SAMUEL 2:1 (MSG)

Hannah continued to express her praise, gratitude and contentment. She appears in only two chapters of the Bible, but we know that she was strong enough to fulfil her promise of dedicating her son to serve God in the temple, seeing him only once a year when she gave him clothes she had made for him. She went on to raise another five children afterwards. The main things Hannah is remembered for are her emotion-soaked prayers of grief and joy and her willingness to dedicate her much-wanted son to God.

Cognitive and creative resilience: Esther

In the book named after her, we read that Esther did not have an easy start to her life. She was an orphan who was brought up by her cousin (2:7). The king announced that he was looking for a new queen, and Esther was among the girls who were brought to the palace for the king to choose from. Esther did not wallow in self-pity and was not consumed by depression. Instead, it seems that she was radiant. She had inner as well as outer beauty and so won favour with everyone – her cousin; Hegai, who was in charge of the harem; the king; and 'everyone who saw her' (2:15). She was wise enough to take advice (2:15), and she was chosen as the new queen.

Esther could have just enjoyed her new life and ignored what was happening in the outside world, but instead she continued to listen to her cousin. He told her when a decree was passed to kill all Jews. Esther had not told anyone at the palace that she was Jewish, so she could have kept quiet and not taken any risks, saving herself but allowing the Jewish people to be slaughtered (although her cousin warned her that she would perish if she did not speak up for the Jews). But Esther heeded her cousin's advice and acted on the belief that she might have been brought to royalty 'for such a time as this' (4:14). She accepted that there might be a larger sense of meaning to her life than she had realised, and she was willing to look beyond her own life to the bigger picture. She courageously agreed to go before the king, despite knowing that people who approached him without being summoned were killed. She problem-solved what she needed to do and concluded, 'If I perish, I perish' (4:16).

Esther made a creative plan. She chose the right clothes for the job, appeared before the king and won his approval. She did not tell the king directly what she wanted at this stage. Far from being impulsive, her problem-solving involved carefully planning the best approach and timing, anticipating what might happen. She invited the king to a banquet. Fanny Fern is credited with coining the saying that 'the way to a man's heart is through his stomach', in the 1800s. Esther may have already worked this out long before, as she arranged a banquet for the king on two consecutive days before revealing her request. At just the right time, she asked the king to spare the Jewish people from destruction, and he agreed.

Despite being a woman in a man's world (where women had no power and her predecessor had been thrown off her throne for saying 'No'), Esther was able to use planning and rhetoric to save not only herself but the Jewish race. She could certainly be described as a resilient woman, who used her mind and creative planning for good.

Hadassah: One night with the king is a novel about the story of Esther.

The author suggests that Esther won the beauty contest not only because of her body, but also because of her mind:

> I retired to my suite in order to work on the last part of my preparations, the one everyone seemed to be overlooking. The *mind*…

> It would take all my youth, all my beauty *and* all my thinking processes and knowledge to give me a chance at being his queen. Toward that end I worked on my state of mind and my soul.[132]

Fiction aside, we know from the facts reported in the biblical account that Esther used planning and creativity. She showed a balance of acceptance and change, as modelled in the famous serenity prayer by Reinhold Niebuhr: 'God grant us the serenity to accept the things we cannot change, the courage to change the things we can, and the wisdom to know the difference.'[133]

This is an aspect of resilience: to change what we can and should, and accept what we cannot change.

Social and systemic resilience: Ruth

Ruth, like Esther, has a short book of the Bible named after her – just four chapters in Ruth's case. By the end of the first chapter, Ruth was in difficult circumstances. Her husband, brother-in-law and father-in-law had all died, although she was young. Without men for provision, the women were in difficulty, as they had no income or protection.

Ruth's mother-in-law Naomi decided to leave Moab and return to her home in the land of Judah. Although Ruth's home was Moab, she chose to accompany Naomi; she had accepted Jewish law and the Jewish religion.

Names are important in this story. Ruth's husband, who died, was called Mahlon, meaning 'sickly' or 'weak'. Mahlon's brother, who also died young, was named Kilion, meaning 'frail' or 'annihilation'. Naomi means 'beautiful grace of God', but she changed her name to Mara, meaning 'bitter'. Ruth means 'friendship'. True to her name, she offered deep friendship to Naomi. They were connected by grief, weeping together (1:9). Ruth promised Naomi:

> Where you go I will go, and where you stay I will stay. Your people will be my people and your God my God. Where you die I will die, and there I will be buried.
> RUTH 1:16–17

When Naomi saw that Ruth was determined, she stopped trying to persuade her to leave (1:18). The Hebrew word for 'determined' here could be translated as 'strengthened herself', a picture of resilience.

Ruth demonstrated the importance of love and support. She left her own home and land. Ruth and Naomi arrived in Bethlehem, which in Hebrew means 'house of bread'. Instead of introducing Ruth to her former neighbours, Naomi told them that she had returned 'empty' (1:21), ignoring the fact that Ruth was with her. Even though Naomi seemed bitter and depressed, Ruth helped Naomi to rebuild her life by staying with her.

The book of Ruth talks about *hesed*, steadfast love. Paul Miller explains that this Hebrew word combines love and loyalty – 'love without an exit strategy'.[134] Such love is desperately needed in our world of broken relationships.

Miller observes:

> Without a male protector, Ruth is sexually vulnerable; without money she is financially destitute; without a friend, she is lonely; and without her country, she is open to prejudice... And she is shouldering the responsibilities of a man. She is one

gutsy lady. Vulnerability is part of the cost of *hesed*. Love carries risk.[135]

Although there had been famine when Naomi first left Bethlehem, when she and Ruth returned the famine was over and the barley harvest was beginning. Ruth set out to make the most of the environment that she found herself in. She honoured Naomi by asking her for permission to work. Naomi did not join her, but Ruth did not complain. Ruth went to the fields to gather up any grain the harvesters left behind, so that she and Naomi could eat, as the Jewish law allowed:

> When you reap the harvest of your land, do not reap to the very edges of your field or gather the gleanings of your harvest. Leave them for the poor and the foreigner.
> LEVITICUS 23:22

Ruth was both poor and a foreigner in Bethlehem, but she was within a culture that made provision for the needy.

Boaz, who owned the field, was touched by Ruth's love for Naomi (2:10–12). He made sure that extra grain was left for Ruth, and he told his men not to touch her, thus protecting and providing for her. Naomi came up with a plan to facilitate Ruth marrying Boaz. An unnamed relative refused to marry Ruth. Wealthy Boaz, whose name means 'strong redeemer', married the poverty-stricken widow Ruth, agreeing to continue Mahlon's line. The elders and the community witnessed this and blessed the couple (4:11–12). Ruth and Boaz had a baby called Obed, who became the grandfather of King David. In this way, Ruth entered the genealogy of Jesus.

Ruth was a resilient woman who knew the importance of relationships, support and love. She made the most of the culture and environment she was in (which provided for the poor). She became a Jewish convert although she was not born a Jew, choosing a new system to commit herself to.

Summary

Each of these five women had a difficult path to walk. They lived in a context in which women had few rights and were expected to rely on men to provide for them. Men could have more than one wife, and masters could sleep with their servants. The king could summon as many women as he wanted for his pleasure. Women without men to protect them (like Ruth and Hagar) could be deemed to be not respectable and were often molested.

Despite the circumstances, each of these five women showed strength and courage. Esther saved the Jewish people from destruction, and Jews still read out her story every year during the festival of Purim, which commemorates these events. The other four women raised sons who influenced history – Jesus, Ishmael (father of the Ishmaelite nation), the prophet Samuel and Obed the grandfather of King David.

In terms of resilience, we remember Mary for her obedience, faith and praise; Hagar for having the strength to move away from a difficult situation and make a fresh start; Hannah for her emotional prayers; Esther for her planning and creativity; and Ruth for her love and for making strong relationship bonds.

Questions

1 Which of the women in this chapter do you most relate to? Why?

2 What examples of resilient women can you think of in the world today?

3 Evaluate your attitude towards women (especially if you are a man). Do you consider women to be as resilient as men? Do you treat them with respect and do what you can to help them flourish and succeed?

4 Apart from the people who are already discussed in this book, can you think of other examples of women and men in the Bible who illustrate spiritual, physical, emotional, cognitive/creative or social/systemic aspects of resilience?

13

Strength in weakness: resilience in the life of Paul

The apostle Paul is not everyone's favourite Bible character. Some people accuse him of complicating the simple message of Jesus; others dislike his attitude towards women, while some feel he condoned slavery. Certainly, Paul could be confrontational and would not have been an easy person to work with, as both Barnabas and Peter discovered (Acts 15:36–39; Galatians 2:11–14).

At the same time, we owe so much to this great man, who was in large measure responsible for the spread of Christianity throughout the Mediterranean world. It is from Paul that we gain our understanding of the major doctrines of our faith. From him we learn about the significance of the cross and resurrection of Jesus, the place of the church in the purposes of God and how to become like Jesus in our everyday lives. And if we want an example of resilience, then we can find almost no better subject than the apostle to the Gentiles.

One incident in particular seems to sum up Paul's resilient attitude towards the many difficulties and trials he faced. In Lystra he was attacked and stoned, dragged outside the city and left for dead.

Then we read, 'But after the disciples had gathered round him, he got up and went back into the city' (Acts 14:20). How remarkable is that? Here is an amazing example of 'bouncing back', of finding the courage to carry on despite fierce opposition. Encouraged by his friends, and strengthened by his faith, Paul found the grace to pick himself up and keep going when it would have been easier to quit.

In 2 Corinthians, we see Paul at his most vulnerable as he opens his heart to his readers about the cost of his ministry. Nowhere else does he speak so candidly about the sufferings he has experienced or his own anxiety and stress. Having established the church in Corinth, Paul had continued onwards to Ephesus and then home to Antioch (Acts 18:1–22). During his absence, other teachers had arrived in the city and not only promoted themselves but also denigrated Paul and his ministry. In his letter, Paul defends himself from their aspersions, not by listing his successes but by revealing his sufferings (2 Corinthians 6:3–10; 11:22–33). Apostolic ministry is authenticated by the willingness to suffer for Christ, not by boasting about one's achievements.

Jars of clay

In the verse at the heart of this epistle, and which provides the foundation of Paul's understanding of Christian ministry, he writes, 'But we have this treasure in jars of clay to show that this all-surpassing power is from God and not from us' (4:7). Here is a great paradox of the Christian life: God has placed his treasure (the life of his Son communicated to us by the Spirit) in the hearts of weak and fallible human beings; God's treasure is wrapped in our humanity. This seems to be a risky strategy, but human weakness in its many expressions is no barrier to the power of God. Indeed, the very fact that God uses people in their weakness shows that it is the power of God at work, and not human ability. His grace will always far surpass our human limitations. Thus, the glory goes to God.

The imagery of jars of clay, or earthen vessels, reminds us that as human beings we are made of dust and therefore are inherently weak and fallible (Genesis 2:7; 3:19). This may be a reference to the small pottery lamps, cheap and fragile, that were readily available in Corinth. More likely it is a reference to the earthenware jars that were commonly used for storage – rough, unglazed, without decoration and easily chipped or cracked. Roman generals returning triumphantly from their campaigns would often conceal their plunder in such unlikely containers.

During World War II in Britain the king ordered that the crown jewels be hidden away to stop them falling into enemy hands. They were placed in a secret vault under the floor in Windsor castle, the location known only to a handful of trusted people. Some of the main jewels were removed from the collection, wrapped in cloth and placed in a biscuit tin for even safer keeping![136] A double bluff, and typically British. That in a sense is what God has done by placing the light of the gospel in our hearts, a most unlikely place to find the power of God at work.

For all his dogged determination and adventurous spirit, Paul was acutely aware of his human limitations and frailty. Early descriptions show him to be an unimpressive figure. *The Acts of Paul* (a non-canonical second-century book), quoted in an article by Stephen Miller, describes a man of medium size whose hair was thinning, his legs a little crooked and his knees far apart. He apparently had large eyes, his bushy eyebrows met in the middle and his nose was somewhat long.[137] In 2 Corinthians, Paul freely acknowledges his emotional turmoil (2:4, 12–13; 7:5–7; 11:28) and sense of inadequacy (2:16; 3:5). He felt the same things that any human being felt; tiredness, pain, confusion and disappointment dogged his steps. He, too, had feet of clay.

Nowhere, however, does Paul suggest that the body is evil or to be despised, but always he is aware of its limitations. He does not deny or suppress his humanity. We too must take note of our 'earthiness', and be aware of our physical, mental and emotional dimensions. The psalmist reminds us that the compassionate God recognises our humanity – he knows how we are formed and remembers that we are dust (Psalm 103:8–16, especially v. 14). God never expects more of us than we can deliver. Resilient people wisely take into account their own humanity and care for themselves accordingly, not to live selfishly or to avoid suffering, but to sustain themselves in the long haul of ministry.

God's all-surpassing power

In the hard realities of apostolic ministry, Paul experienced the power of God at work in him so that he was not overwhelmed by his sufferings. Yes, his struggles were great, but the power of God at work within him was even greater. He continues writing with an honest description of the contrasts within his experience: 'We are hard pressed on every side, but not crushed; perplexed, but not in despair; persecuted, but not abandoned; struck down, but not destroyed' (4:8–9).

Whatever challenges he faced, the power of God enabled him to come through them in the end. Indeed, it was as if the death and resurrection of Jesus was being played out in his life, time and time again (4:10–11). The more he suffered, the more the life of Christ worked through him to bless others: 'So then, death is at work in us, but life is at work in you' (4:12).

This is a principle that underlies all effective Christian ministry and one that we must be aware of if we are to be resilient in the face of hardships. Jesus himself spoke about it clearly when he said, 'Very truly I tell you, unless a grain of wheat falls to the ground and dies, it remains only a single seed. But if it dies, it produces many seeds' (John 12:24). There is always a price to be paid for spiritual fruitfulness. When we realise this, we are not surprised when we too experience difficulties. We know that, weak as we are, the power of

God at work in us will also bring us through triumphantly in the end. Our sufferings will lead to blessing for others.

Asian nightmare

As he writes to his friends in Corinth, Paul identifies two situations when he had been at his lowest point but, through God, had found the strength to continue. The first happened in the province of Asia (modern-day Turkey), and although the details are sketchy, the trauma of it is clear. He writes, 'We were under great pressure, far beyond our ability to endure, so that we despaired of life itself. Indeed, we felt we had received the sentence of death' (1:8–9). This was no ordinary hardship or difficulty. Even on the scale of Paul's experience, this was out of the ordinary, a terrifying ordeal where he genuinely felt his life might be at an end.

At the height of the crisis two things happened. To begin with, he and his friends found themselves cast upon God like never before. God became their only hope: 'But this happened that we might not rely on ourselves but on God, who raises the dead' (1:9). Then, when all seemed lost, they experienced a miraculous deliverance, that could only have come from God and that also assured them of future security: 'He has delivered us from such a deadly peril, and he will deliver us again.' (1:10). God seems to allow situations to arise that expose our own inability to cope and cause us to grow in our dependency upon him. We are never stronger than when we are most conscious of our own inadequacy yet leaning on the dependability of God in any and every circumstance.

Reflecting on this experience, Paul recognises that a significant factor in their deliverance had been the prayers of the Corinthians. 'On him we have set our hope,' he writes, 'that he will continue to deliver us, as you help us by your prayers. Then many will give thanks on our behalf for the gracious favour granted us in answer to the prayers of many' (1:10–11). We should never underestimate the power of prayer, nor the importance of surrounding ourselves with people who will pray for us. This is perhaps one of the most undervalued factors in resilience – the power of praying friends.

Comfort

One of the good things to come out of Paul's Asian trauma (and his suffering in general) is a deeper understanding of how God comes to our aid in such times, and how we can use our experience to help others facing difficulties. After the customary greetings at the start of the letter, Paul begins with a burst of praise that reveals his thinking and shows what we might call the 'comfort cycle':

> Praise be to the God and Father of our Lord Jesus Christ, the Father of compassion and the God of all comfort, who comforts us in all our troubles, so that we can comfort those in any trouble with the comfort we ourselves have received from God.
> 2 CORINTHIANS 1:3–4

Here we see how comfort cascades down from God to us, and then on to others, thus increasing their resilience as well.

As far as Paul is concerned, God is the source of all comfort. He is not aloof or distant, unfeeling and uncaring. The God whom Paul serves is one who feels for us in our trials and who by his Spirit communicates to us the comfort we need to get through our troubles. The word used for comfort here is *paraklesis*, from the same Greek word used for the Holy Spirit as the comforter in John 14:16. The idea is of one who draws alongside us to help us in our time of need. While the Spirit consoles and soothes us, healing our wounds, he also fortifies us for the challenge and enables us to rise up again and meet the obstacle before us with renewed faith and vigour. Philip Hughes comments, 'No matter how great the sufferings a Christian is called to endure, they are matched, and more than matched, by the comfort which God bestows.'[138]

Having received God's comfort into our own lives, we are then equipped to help others who are facing difficulty. We are able to comfort others simply because we ourselves have been in need and have found in God the strength to cope. By our testimony, words of encouragement and practical help, we are enabled to support others experiencing trials so that they may also overcome. 'Our lives are like a goblet,' says experienced pastor Paul Mallard. 'First suffering flows in and then comfort flows in. Then, out from our lives flow the comforts that just flowed in. So, our lives become a source of blessing and help to those around us.'[139] Understanding that God has a purpose for us even in our suffering greatly enhances our resilience. When we see how God not only comes to our own aid, but how he can use our pain to help others, we are strengthened in our faith.

The mysterious thorn

The second situation Paul refers to in which he had been battered and baffled, and yet found the strength to carry on, is mentioned in 12:7–10. He writes, 'To keep me from becoming conceited, I was given a thorn in my flesh, a messenger of Satan, to torment me' (v. 7). Scholars have sought to identify exactly what caused his suffering, but it remains unclear. It might have been migraines, eye problems, epilepsy or malaria. He may have been referring to the constant harassment he received from his Jewish opponents, some demonic interference or even a particular individual, such as Alexander (2 Timothy 4:14). We cannot be certain, and it is perhaps better that it is not specified. The thorn can then represent any attack upon us that might destabilise our faith and threaten our well-being.

What we can say is that the thorn was probably physical (it is 'in the flesh'), it was very personal (something specific to him as a person) and it was extremely painful (the word 'thorn' refers to a sharp wooden stake). It may have been a direct demonic attack on Paul ('a messenger of Satan'). Certainly, the devil used it against him – perhaps whispering in his ear words of condemnation, accusing him of lacking faith and needling him incessantly to give up altogether, tormenting him mentally and spiritually.

Without doubt Paul wanted to get rid of this affliction and did everything within his power and know-how to set himself free. As always, he turned to God for help: 'Three times I pleaded with the Lord to take it away from me' (v. 8). This pleading refers to earnest, urgent, intercessory prayer. It wasn't just that he prayed once, but three times, indicating different seasons of fervent prayer by which he sought deliverance from the situation. In all likelihood, he not only prayed and fasted himself, but enlisted the support of other prayer warriors too, but all to no avail. Eventually, worn out and confused, he sank to his knees not only battered, but baffled as well.

And then God spoke. Into the silence of his bewilderment came the healing word of the Lord – 'But he said to me' (v. 9). When he had no more prayers to pray and when his natural strength had been exhausted, then he heard the still, small voice of God. How gracious it is of God to speak to us in our times of need and at just the right moment. He doesn't put us through the mill for the fun of it, but so that his good purpose for us can be accomplished. When God saw that Paul's pride had been dealt with, then he spoke to him a word of life, a word that not only strengthened Paul but which has continued to strengthen God's embattled people down the centuries.

First came a liberating promise: 'My grace is sufficient for you' (v. 9) – six short words of remarkable depth and power, bringing reassurance and hope, not just for Paul but for us also. God's grace in this instance is the impartation of divine strength into our human weakness, enabling us to do more than we ever imagined possible and giving us the faith to endure in the midst of our trials. Such grace is always sufficient – that is, just the right amount to enable us to cope with our particular circumstances, always enough and always adequate for our situation, and always available to us no matter where we find ourselves. What relief must have flooded his soul! The pain was still there, the challenge remained, and yet now the apostle knew he could not only endure it but also overcome it (Romans 8:37–39). This same grace is available to all God's people today, in equal measure and with similar effect. If God does not remove the difficulty, he will most certainly give us the strength to endure it, and to do so with joy.

Then came the revelation of an abiding principle: 'for my power is made perfect in weakness' (v. 9). This reminds us of the treasure in earthen vessels and confirms the thought that our weakness is not a hindrance to the flow of God's power. Indeed, God's power is best seen or displayed in the context of human weakness. When we see how frail, flawed and fragile the messenger is, we have to conclude that the power must belong to God. Our natural human strength can actually inhibit the flow of God's life through us. When we are strong, confident and capable, with no sense of weakness or inadequacy, we are likely to try to accomplish things in our own strength. This robs God of his glory and stifles his ability to use us. This is why God often leaves an area of weakness in our lives that is unresolved, because it makes room for him to work both in us and through us.

Strengthened by hearing the clear voice of God, Paul responds with renewed hope and joy: 'Therefore I will boast all the more gladly about my weaknesses, so that Christ's power may rest on me' (v. 9). Paul now sees that his weakness is not a liability but an opportunity for him to experience more of God's power in his life, a power that will rest gently upon him in his weakness. There is no need to be ashamed of weakness, no cause to hide it away from view. Human limitations leave room for God to work.

A conviction now takes hold of Paul's heart and shapes his thinking, a truth that runs contrary to all natural assumptions: 'When I am weak, then I am strong' (v. 10). This revelation turns human thinking upside down. The resilience we speak of as Christians is not about getting stronger and stronger so that there is no challenge we cannot face. No, it is about allowing God to transcend our weaknesses with his all-sufficient grace and power. If we are resilient, it is not because we are strong people but because we allow God to be strong in our weakness.

Another type of angel?

The great Chinese Christian leader Watchman Nee shared how as a young believer he aspired to be the perfect Christian, one who had no cares or concerns and who would smile from morning to night. He would be bold, unafraid and courageous in every situation and never feel sad or know defeat. Anything less would mean he was not victorious but a failure. Then one day he read 2 Corinthians and saw that Paul was sorrowful. He writes:

> I asked, 'Was Paul sorrowful?' I read that he shed many tears. I asked, 'Did Paul cry?' I read that Paul suffered and was sad. I asked, 'Did Paul suffer, and was he sad?' I read that he was burdened and despaired even of his life. I asked, 'Did Paul despair?' As I continued reading, I saw that there were many things of which I had never thought. I had never considered that a person like Paul would have these problems. I began to realise that Christians are not another type of angel. God has not put a race of angels on the earth and said, 'These are Christians.' I also began to see that Paul was very close to us; he was not so far off. Paul was someone I know; he was not a stranger. I know him because I saw that he was a man.[140]

Part of Paul's legacy to us is permission to recognise our own humanity and to be comfortable with weakness, fallibility and limitation. It is the understanding that God has chosen to work through us as we are, placing his treasure in our fragile human vessels. It is the knowledge that however weak we are, God's power is greater still and he will enable us to endure difficulty and accomplish the task he has given us. This is the way of resilience.

Questions

1 What do you understand now about Paul's statement that 'we have this treasure in jars of clay' (2 Corinthians 4:7)? How does this aid our resilience?

2 Have you ever been able to comfort others because you have been through something similar and found comfort yourself?

3 Do you have a 'thorn in the flesh'? What does it mean to know that God's grace is sufficient for you?

4 What is your attitude to weakness, in yourself or in others? How does Paul's teaching transform the way we look at weakness?

5 Pray that you may know the power of Christ gently resting on you, even in your weakness.

14

Jesus, our model for resilience and endurance

We have now considered several examples of resilience through the Bible characters we have studied, and this helps to ground the principles of resilience in real human lives. These people were just like us, and if they endured, so can we. The supreme example of resilience, however, is to be seen in Jesus, and it is to an examination of his life that we now turn.

Writing in order to encourage Jewish converts to keep believing despite the pressures they were under, the author of the book of Hebrews urges them to follow the example of Jesus when it comes to endurance. They were in danger of drifting away, letting go of their grip on God and throwing away their confidence. Some had already stopped meeting for fellowship, while others were once more tangled in sin. Here is his message to them:

> Therefore, since we are surrounded by such a great cloud of witnesses, let us throw off everything that hinders and the sin that so easily entangles. And let us run with perseverance the race marked out for us, fixing our eyes on Jesus, the pioneer and perfecter of faith. For the joy that was set before him he endured the cross, scorning its shame, and sat down at the

right hand of the throne of God. Consider him who endured such opposition from sinners, so that you will not grow weary and lose heart.

HEBREWS 12:1-3

The dangers are clearly identified: to come under the power of sin again, and to give way to exhaustion and discouragement. These are clear and present dangers no matter where or when we live. The answer remains the same as well: we are to be encouraged by the examples of those who have gone before us in the faith (the cloud of witnesses), and to refuse to lose heart (see Hebrews 11). More importantly, we are to fix our eyes on Jesus. Whatever the pressures, whatever the distractions, we are to look away to Jesus and concentrate our gaze on him. Such a preoccupation with Jesus will not only cure the malady of soul that may threaten to overtake us, but it will also inspire us to keep running the race set before us.

Athletic contests were popular throughout the ancient world, and the New Testament writers turn frequently to the sporting arena to illustrate the qualities needed in living the Christian life (Acts 20:24; 1 Corinthians 9:24-27; Galatians 5:7; 2 Timothy 4:7). Just as an athlete needs grit and determination to run the race, so believers need perseverance (Greek: *hupomone*) as they follow Christ on the path he has marked out for their lives. Yet how easy it is to give up! The antidote is to consider Jesus, to think more deeply about his life and example, and to find in him the motivation we need to keep going.

Opposition and persecution

Although the ministry of Jesus was only three short years, it was packed with incident and challenge. From the beginning, Satan and the powers of darkness sought to test him and divert him from his calling. The temptations in the wilderness came as he began his public ministry and tested him as to how he would go about his work. By questioning Jesus' identity as God's Son, Satan sought to rob him of his confidence, yet Jesus did not yield (Matthew 4:1–11). At the same time, the religious leaders of the day were quick to oppose him. Their initial jealousy at his success and popularity soon escalated into outright hostility and murderous intent to stop him. Wherever he went, they dogged his steps and sought to catch him out, discouraging others from following him and using underhanded means to discredit him. They slandered him with accusations of being demon-possessed and charged him with blasphemy. Eventually their wicked schemes would lead to his arrest and crucifixion. (See Luke 5:21; 7:30; 11:53–54; 19:47–48; Mark 3:6; 11:18; Matthew 12:14.)

Desertion and rejection

Jesus had to live with the demands and expectations of the crowds who gathered around him. He attracted a huge following, and it was hard for him to be alone. Many saw him as a political messiah, one who would overthrow the Romans; others regarded him as a miracle worker who would meet their needs. Finally, when he refused to acquiesce to their demands to be their king, many deserted him (John 6:15, 66). Jesus knew the disappointment of losing followers, but he had never based his ministry on any external marker of success, such as popularity.

Much harder to cope with would have been the hostility from his family members. His own brothers did not believe in him, and this must have hurt him deeply (Mark 3:20–21; John 7:3–5). Likewise, the violent rejection he experienced in his home town of Nazareth – given all they had seen and heard from him – must have saddened him. In the clamour that followed he could well have been seriously hurt (Matthew 13:53–58; Luke 4:28–30). John sums up the pain of rejection that Jesus had to handle like this: 'He came to that which was his own, but his own did not receive him' (John 1:11).

Grief and loss

There were deeply painful times as well for the one described as the man of sorrows (Isaiah 53:3). He was close to his cousin John the Baptist, and when John was imprisoned and subsequently beheaded, his death affected Jesus greatly, for he had lost an ally and friend (Matthew 14:3-13). Likewise, the death of his friend Lazarus and the pain of Mary and Martha brought him to tears, even though he knew that God would bring Lazarus back to life (John 11:33-37). As he surveyed the city of Jerusalem, he wept over it, saddened by the refusal of its people to believe (Luke 19:41-44). Jesus was a real human being, with feelings and emotions. He felt these things deeply and could easily have been overwhelmed, but he was not. He found the strength to keep moving forward.

Disappointment and betrayal

As the last week of his life began, two huge disappointments awaited Jesus. First, the betrayal by Judas – and that by a kiss, a sign of affection and love, and for monetary gain. Jesus knew from the start who would betray him, but still found grace to love Judas, wash his feet along with the others and break bread with him during the Passover meal. How deep the pain of a friend's betrayal! (See John 6:64; 13:18, 26-27; Luke 22:1-5; Matthew 26:47-50.)

Second came Peter's denial of ever having known Jesus – not once, but three times, and so soon after his protestation of absolute loyalty. Peter, the disciple in whom Jesus had placed such trust and shown such belief. His boastful self-confidence quickly melted away when confronted over his association with Jesus (Mark 14:27-31; Luke 22:31-32, 54-62). Jesus knew what had happened and must have felt badly let down, yet still forgave Peter (John 21:15-19).

Suffering

Jesus never flinched from the prospect of crucifixion. With bravery and great courage, he had determinedly set his face towards Jerusalem as the end drew near, resolutely accepting the fate that awaited him (Luke 9:51; 13:22; Mark 10:32). Three times he graphically informed his disciples of the fate that awaited him there (Mark 8:31–32; 9:30–32; 10:33–34). If he appeared to hesitate in the garden of Gethsemane, it was but a momentary pause to take stock of what the cross would mean for him. He did not go to the cross lightly. The prospect of suffering for the sin of the world rightly troubled him deeply: 'My soul is overwhelmed with sorrow to the point of death,' he admitted (Matthew 26:38). When he needed his friends, they fell asleep. His resolve soon took over again, however, as with great courage he offered himself to do the Father's will: 'Not my will, but yours be done,' he prayed (Luke 22:42).

The shadow of the cross loomed large in the life of Jesus, and this is the event to which the writer of Hebrews draws our attention: he 'endured the cross, scorning its shame' (12:2). Here we are reminded of the physical aspect of his suffering, experiencing one of the most painful forms of execution ever invented, and the psychological dimension, the shame that went with it – the public humiliation and embarrassment, the mockery and ridicule that were heaped upon him as he died an innocent man, wrongly accused. Added to this we are reminded of the emotional pain of his rejection by those he had come to save: he 'endured such opposition from sinners' (12:3), a phrase summarising the hostility vented upon him by those who watched him die.

The life of Jesus, and in particular his death on the cross, are set before us as an example of endurance, a model of resilience. We have seen the challenges that he faced, but what were his resources? How was it that Jesus could keep going until the very end when he uttered that triumphant cry, 'It is finished' (John 19:30)? What were the sources of his resilience?

Sent by the Father

Without doubt a major factor for Jesus was his strong sense of calling, of having been sent into the world by the Father for a particular reason and purpose. This gave him his vocation, his mission for living, and filled his life with meaning. As we have seen earlier, these are all key factors in resilience. The knowledge that what we are doing is important fortifies us to keep going. From boyhood, Jesus lived with the desire to be about his Father's business, and this consciousness of a divine calling intensified and clarified with the passing of time (Luke 2:49). Time and again in John's gospel we see Jesus referring to the fact that he had been 'sent' from God, not to please himself but to do the Father's will (3:17; 5:30; 6:38; 7:28–29; 8:29). This awareness of a higher calling enabled him to keep his focus and not be distracted. He spoke often of the 'work' that he had been given to do, and that he was determined to finish (John 4:34; 5:36; 9:4; 17:4; 18:37). He was motivated and energised by this strong, inner sense of constraint.

Speaking one day in the synagogue at Nazareth, he opened the scroll of the prophet Isaiah to some verses that were central to his understanding of his task and his calling: 'The Spirit of the Lord is on me, because he has anointed me to proclaim good news to the poor' (Luke 4:18–19, referring to Isaiah 61:1–2). This was the mandate for his mission and the focus of his earthly life. He expressed it through his teaching; by healing the sick and delivering those oppressed by the devil; in his compassion towards the needy; and through the way he treated those marginalised by society. Jesus knew what he was about. Resilient people are characterised as possessing a clear vision and aim in life.

The beloved

Allied to this sense of calling was a strong sense of identity. When Jesus came to John for baptism, a voice from heaven declared unequivocally, 'This is my Son, whom I love; with him I am well pleased' (Matthew 3:17). Even as he began his ministry, and before he had done anything to merit such a status, the Father bore witness to his true identity. Later, on the mount of transfiguration, as the time for his death drew near, the heavenly voice spoke again: 'This is my Son, whom I love; with him I am well pleased. Listen to him!' (Matthew 17:5). As he prepared for his greatest challenge, he was again strengthened by the reminder that he was the object of the Father's love. People who know their true identity, who know they are loved by God unconditionally and without reservation, have an inner stability that helps them through difficult times. Those whose identity is carried within themselves, and is not based on external criteria, tend to be more resolute and less easily swayed by changing events and fortunes. (See Romans 8:35–39.)

Communion with God

Brennan Manning writes, 'A central theme in the personal life of Jesus Christ, which lies at the very heart of the revelation that he is, is his growing intimacy with, trust in, and love of his Abba.'[141] Solitude was vital to this, and we often find Jesus withdrawing from the crowds in order to be alone (Mark 1:35; Matthew 13:1; Luke 5:16; John 11:54). Doubtless this was to refresh his soul from the pressures he was under. Even the most extrovert of people need times when they can rest and be refreshed, both physically and spiritually. More important than that, however, was Jesus' desire to spend time with the Father, listening for his voice and sensing his direction (John 5:19, 30; 8:28; 12:49). This deep inner life of communion with God was what fortified him and kept him going. As David Runcorn puts it, 'In those lonely places the deep springs of the Spirit's life renewed him, the Father's will strengthened him and the Father's love inspired him.'[142] We too must develop our relationship with God if we are to stay strong in the midst of the demands of life and ministry.

Prayer and scripture

Jesus made it a habit to worship on the sabbath (Luke 4:16). Not surprisingly, prayer was a vital ingredient in his life, a regular discipline of depending on God (Luke 5:16; 9:18; Matthew 14:23; Mark 6:46). He prayed before he made major decisions (Luke 6:12), and at moments of real challenge (Luke 9:28; Matthew 14:13; 26:36). Likewise, the scriptures were foundational to his inner strength. He was nourished by the word of God, and it was his knowledge of the scriptures that helped him resist the temptations of Satan in the wilderness (Matthew 4:4, 7, 10). He was able to quote widely from the Old Testament because he was at home there, and could interpret its message wisely to his hearers (Luke 24:25–27, 45–47). We may be tempted to think that worship, prayer and scripture reading are of little consequence, but over time, and with discipline, they help to form the bedrock of a strong and stable spiritual life that greatly enhances our resilience.

Friends

Jesus surrounded himself with good friends and people who supported him. Even he did not live in social isolation with no need for human companionship or support. The disciples provided a major source of attachment for him, and he was not ashamed to call them his friends (John 15:14). Out of the twelve disciples, Peter, John and James seem to have formed a more intimate circle (Luke 9:28; Mark 5:37–43; Matthew 26:37–46), with John – the beloved disciple – as the closest of all (John 13:23; 19:26; 20:2; 21:7, 20). Jesus seemed to have found particular comfort from his friendship with Lazarus and his sisters Mary and Martha. Their home in Bethany provided a safe place, where he was always welcome and could relax (Luke 10:38–42; John 11:1–6; Matthew 21:17). In addition, a group of wealthy women travelled with Jesus and supported him financially, and perhaps practically as well (Luke 8:1–3; John 19:25). When we recognise how much Jesus valued these friendships, we are reminded that building a good support network is vital for each of us if we are to maintain our resilience. Those who are isolated tend not to thrive as well as those who receive regular encouragement and help from others.

Self-care

It may seem surprising to realise that Jesus practised what we would now call appropriate self-care. He gave attention to his own well-being, not in a self-protective way but in order to ensure he could fulfil the work he had been given to do. He maintained certain personal boundaries in the face of the constant, daily demands upon him and his time. Although he was always willing to be interrupted, he was also not afraid to set limits. As we mentioned in chapter 4, Jesus knew when to say 'No' – even to the needs, even to the opportunities (Mark 1:35–38; Luke 4:42–44; 5:15–16; Mark 7:24; 9:30). Boundaries should never be rigid or unyielding, but people who live without limits fare less well when it comes to personal well-being and run the risk of burnout or compassion fatigue.

Jesus protected his inner life and his communion with God despite his busyness (Mark 6:45–46; Luke 9:18; 11:1). As we have seen, he observed the sabbath, not in a legalistic way like the Pharisees, but in a way that provided rest and the opportunity to worship (Luke 4:16). He took time to sleep (Mark 4:38) and knew how to relax, often joining with others for meals, where he 'reclined at the table' (Luke 7:36; 11:37; 14:1; 22:14). Life as an itinerant preacher provided plenty of opportunity for walking and healthy exercise. He thought about his physical safety, too, and was never foolhardy in exposing himself to unnecessary danger. When his life was under threat he sometimes hid himself until the time was right to move about more publicly (John 7:1; 8:59; 11:54; 12:36). When we recognise that Jesus took such measures, we are freed to invest in our own well-being without feeling guilty or selfish.

Joy set before him

Inevitably, the time came when Jesus had to move towards Jerusalem and face the reality that his God-given mission would call for him to lay down his life for others. This transition, from his ministry mainly in Galilee to his arrival in Jerusalem, is marked quite clearly in Luke's gospel: 'As the time approached for him to be taken up to heaven, Jesus resolutely set out for Jerusalem' (Luke 9:51; see also 13:22; 17:11; 18:31; 19:28). Jesus met the inevitability of his death with a courageous determination not to avoid the cross. His motivation, according to Hebrews, was not some heroic death wish but was based on 'the joy that was set before him' (12:2). The joyful anticipation of future reward, or of the achievement of a desired outcome, is a great boost to perseverance, and it was a significant factor in the determination with which Jesus approached the climax of his ministry.

Doing the Father's will

Jesus' joy centred on doing the Father's will and finishing the task he had been given. He was aware of all that lay before him and told his disciples exactly what to expect (Mark 8:31–32; 9:30–32; 10:33–34). He knew that suffering awaited him, and it disturbed him, yet he did not flinch: 'Now my soul is troubled, and what shall I say? "Father, save me from this hour"? No, it was for this very reason I came to this hour. Father, glorify your name!' (John 12:27–28). His aim was to glorify the Father, and that he would do by giving his life on the cross. In this he delighted, and it fortified him. This was the charge he had received from the Father, and to obey him in this way gave him pleasure: 'The reason my Father loves me is that I lay down my life – only to take it up again. No one takes it from me, but I lay it down of my own accord' (John 10:17–18). This very thought gave nobility to his sacrifice and strengthened his resolve.

Blessing others

Jesus understood that his death was the way by which salvation could come to the whole world, and that his death would benefit others: 'the Son of Man did not come to be served, but to serve, and to give his life as a ransom for many' (Mark 10:45). He was the good shepherd, laying down his life out of love for his sheep, and he gladly took that role (John 10:11). The knowledge that his death would bring blessing to many motivated him to offer his life joyfully. There would be a result, an outcome by which he would be satisfied, and the prospect of such a reward strengthened his resolve. 'Very truly I tell you, unless a grain of wheat falls to the ground and dies, it remains only a single seed,' he said. 'But if it dies, it produces many seeds' (John 12:24).

Trust and faith

Jesus went to the cross trusting in his Father's wisdom, power and love. As he died on the cross, he entrusted himself to God. He cried out with a loud voice, 'Father, into your hands I commit my spirit' (Luke 23:46; see also 1 Peter 2:23). He plunged himself into the darkness of death, knowing the Father would catch him and that he would come out the other side victorious; but it was still a leap of faith, an act of courageous trust. This willingness to trust in God, even in the darkness, can be the basis for our own resilience.

Furthermore, Jesus believed in resurrection, and that death could be defeated. He knew he would suffer, but he also knew he would rise again. Each time he warned his disciples of his coming death he told them clearly he would rise again after three days, but they could not grasp it (Mark 8:31; 9:31; 10:34). He also spoke about it during the cleansing of the temple (John 2:19–22). This knowledge that God is a God who raises the dead – who delivers us from seemingly impossible situations – can give us hope when all seems lost. This was Paul's experience in Asia, as we saw in chapter 13, and it can be ours as well.

Back to the Father

Part of the joy set before Jesus was not only the belief that he would come through death and rise again, but that subsequently he would return to the Father's side. This hope was within him even as he spoke to his disciples in the upper room: 'I came from the Father and entered the world; now I am leaving the world and going back to the Father' (John 16:28). The way home would lead through the cross, and would be a painful and lonely path to tread, but the thought of being reunited with the Father was ever before him. After the resurrection he would ascend to heaven and then be exalted at the Father's right hand, his work completed and the victory won (Acts 1:9–11; 2:32–33; Hebrews 1:3). We are to fix our eyes on him as he is now, seated triumphantly at the right hand of the throne of God (Hebrews 12:2). Seeing him there, in the place of authority and rule, as the one who has conquered and overcome, will give us great confidence to believe that he will also help us to overcome our struggles.

Jesus is described as the 'pioneer and perfecter of faith' (Hebrews 12:2). The word 'pioneer' suggests that he is the originator of our faith, the one who brings it into being, much as an author conceives a novel and brings it to birth. The word 'perfecter' suggests he is the one who brings our faith to completion, to maturity – he is the finisher. This suggests that Jesus is watching over us, and working so that our faith will not fail but will be strengthened so that we can endure. When we put these two titles together, we find grounds for believing that we can persevere in our faith. As Thomas Hewitt comments on this verse, 'The thought here is that he who begins a good work within the believer will certainly bring it to triumphant issue.'[143]

Because Jesus overcame the world, so can we (John 16:33). Whatever the race marked out for us, we know we can run it with perseverance because Jesus himself runs with us. He is the great example of resilience and the source of our own ability to endure.

Questions

1 The writer to the Hebrews uses a metaphor from athletics. What examples of resilience have you seen as you have watched or taken part in sport? Why do sportspeople need to be resilient?

2 Are you surprised when you read about the many challenges that Jesus faced and their impact upon him? Although he was fully God, he was also fully human and felt all the things that we feel. How does this encourage you? Read Hebrews 4:14–16.

3 Of the different sources given for the endurance of Jesus, which stand out for you, and why?

4 How in particular did the cross demonstrate the courage and resilience of Jesus?

5 What will it mean for you to 'fix your eyes' on Jesus and to 'consider him'?

15

Conclusion: building a more resilient life

Growing through adversity

We began this book with definitions of resilience, which referred to a response to adversity, pressures or difficulties. In order to become resilient, we need to experience challenging times. It is through facing those challenges that we develop mental toughness.

A butterfly needs to struggle to get out of the chrysalis. If someone helps it out, it will probably never be able to fly, because the butterfly needs the struggle to strengthen its wings. Similarly, we need to struggle to become stronger as people. We need to allow children and others we care about to experience their own struggles so that they can grow strong; overprotecting them can restrict their development.

Developing deep roots

Tim Herbert, who provides care for people in ministry and who is also a gardener, has described the importance of people developing deep roots, just as trees need to. He has given permission for us to include his description here, which draws together several of the themes in this book:

> How could [the apostle Paul] be stoned and left for dead one day, and the next day go to the neighbouring town and carry on preaching the gospel (Acts 14:19–21)?

> Paul had deep roots. He was utterly convinced of God's love for him despite such trials (Romans 8:38–39).He was completely persuaded of the need for humanity to hear the gospel (1 Corinthians 9:16), and death held no fear for him because he knew what would happen to him after he died (Philippians 1:20–24). This enabled him to keep his suffering in perspective – it was nothing compared to what Christ had suffered for him.

> How do we develop these deep roots? To use a sapling as an analogy, trees develop deep roots by going through hardship in the first place. We know that we need to stake a young tree to stop it blowing over in the first place, but what most of us do not know is that if we stake it too tightly, it… will not develop deep roots. Only if it's allowed to wave in the wind will its roots go deeper into the ground to provide more stability. The more it shakes, the further the roots will go seeking rocks to hang on to. For us, those rocks are God, and the great truths of our salvation. When the storm strikes, our response should not be to doubt our calling, or to wonder why God did not help us when we needed him. It should be to confess our trust in him despite our outward circumstances, as many of the psalms do… the psalmist reorientates himself back to trusting in God as he reconciles his belief in God with his difficult circumstance, either by confessing faith in the midst of adversity or by turning his accusation into a prayer for deliverance. Having done this, he puts down deeper roots, finding greater stability and life-giving nutrients which will sustain him when the next disaster strikes.[144]

We need to hold on to biblical truths, the rocks we can cling to as we grow deep roots. We could add roots to our diagram of resilience in chapter 10. If we are strong in the spiritual domain, we will develop roots that go deep into the soil and help us remain stable.

Spiritual factors as the key to resilience

Barrett and Martin state:

> Resilient people have an approach to life that is characterised by realistic optimism, self-confidence, a sense of humour, the ability to stay focused under pressure, not being easily defeated by failure and finding meaning even in negative experiences. They often have a track record of dealing successfully with stressful situations.[145]

We have added to this list further spiritual, physical, emotional, cognitive, creative, social and systemic contributors to resilience. You can use the rating scale in Appendix A to assess your current resilience in these domains.

Each domain is important, but the spiritual aspects of resilience are key. You may have noticed that towards the end of the chapters on physical, emotional, cognitive and social aspects of resilience we returned to spiritual factors. We cannot divorce the other elements from spirituality.

If we are spiritually strong, we can have inner resilience (and deep roots) even if our body and mind fail and we lack support. As it says in 2 Corinthians 4:16, 'Though outwardly we are wasting away, yet inwardly we are being renewed day by day.' Or, as Jesus put it, 'The spirit is willing, but the flesh is weak' (Mark 14:38).

I have a friend who is in her 90s and has significant problems with thinking and memory (cognitive), is frail in body (physical) and whose loved ones have passed away (social). Despite all of this, in my eyes she is resilient as she continues to trust God for today and for eternity (spiritual), and so she is not anxious or afraid (emotional). A sense of meaning, trust in God's mercy and hope of eternal life are the keys that can help as we face the death of loved ones and our own mortality.

If I could choose just one domain to be resilient in, I would choose the spiritual. Resilience is not my main goal in life. My goal is to love and obey God and to love others. As I do this, my spiritual resilience will increase. We should rely on God, not on our own strength and strategies, because 'it is God who works in you to will and to act in order to fulfil his good purpose' (Philippians 2:13).

Thankfully, we do not have to choose just one of these domains. We can do all we can (with God's help) to be as resilient as we can in the spiritual, physical, emotional, cognitive and creative, and social and systemic areas. This is good stewardship and enables us to be effective for God as long as he enables us, and resilient for his glory.

Questions

1   This book mentions examples of various people being resilient in traumatic situations, including hostage situations, prison or concentration camps, paralysis, the aftermath of genocide and extreme poverty. We have also considered a range of Bible characters. Did any particular example stand out to you? If so, which, and why?

2   If you have completed the rating scale twice, have there been any changes? Do you think you have changed over the time you have been reading this book?

3   Although Jesus lived in a society that was sometimes hostile, he remained resilient throughout his earthly life. If you like, you

could try using the rating scale to assess Jesus' resilience in the five domains. What do you notice?

4 If you could only be resilient in one domain, which would you choose – spiritual, physical, emotional, cognitive and creative, or social and systemic resilience?

5 What goal will you set yourself to increase your resilience over the coming months?

Appendix A

Resilience rating scale

Please rate each item using the following scale:

1 = NEVER

2 = RARELY

3 = SOMETIMES

4 = OFTEN

5 = ALWAYS

There are no right or wrong answers. Make sure that you answer every question, so that you can compare your scores for the subsections.

Spiritual resilience (see chapter 2)

1 My life has a sense of meaning or purpose.

1	2	3	4	5

2 I am following a sense of calling or vocation.

1	2	3	4	5

3 I have hope for the future.

1	2	3	4	5

4 I forgive others and myself.

1	2	3	4	5

5 I practise gratitude.

1	2	3	4	5

6 I take a day of rest each week ('sabbath time').

1	2	3	4	5

7 I pray every day.

1	2	3	4	5

8 I have times of meditation or listening to God in stillness/silence.

1	2	3	4	5

9 I am part of a caring church fellowship or other community that shares my beliefs and values.

1	2	3	4	5

10 I have a strong faith in God.

1	2	3	4	5

Physical resilience (see chapter 4)

11 I have a good level of physical activity (e.g. 150 minutes a week of moderate exercise, or 75 minutes a week of vigorous exercise).

| 1 | 2 | 3 | 4 | 5 |

12 I get enough sleep and have a good energy level.

| 1 | 2 | 3 | 4 | 5 |

13 I avoid overworking and I take adequate time to rest (on a daily and weekly basis).

| 1 | 2 | 3 | 4 | 5 |

14 I take enough holidays, and allow margin in my life.

| 1 | 2 | 3 | 4 | 5 |

15 My weight is in the healthy range.

| 1 | 2 | 3 | 4 | 5 |

16 I have a healthy, balanced diet.

| 1 | 2 | 3 | 4 | 5 |

17 I drink fewer than 14 units of alcohol weekly.

| 1 | 2 | 3 | 4 | 5 |

18 I care for my health, including being careful about my use of medication.

| 1 | 2 | 3 | 4 | 5 |

19 I cope well when I experience health problems or pain.

| 1 | 2 | 3 | 4 | 5 |

20 I make time to go outside and enjoy the natural world.

| 1 | 2 | 3 | 4 | 5 |

Emotional resilience (see chapter 6)

21 I feel able to cope.

| 1 | 2 | 3 | 4 | 5 |

22 I have effective strategies for managing stress.

| 1 | 2 | 3 | 4 | 5 |

23 I give my anxieties to God, letting go of my worries instead of ruminating on them.

| 1 | 2 | 3 | 4 | 5 |

24 The way I express my emotions is reasonable in the circumstances and not an overreaction.

| 1 | 2 | 3 | 4 | 5 |

25 I avoid unhealthy ways of dealing with feelings (e.g. self-harm, excessive caffeine or smoking, or addictions).

| 1 | 2 | 3 | 4 | 5 |

26 I remain calm under pressure.

| 1 | 2 | 3 | 4 | 5 |

27 It takes a lot to make me feel frightened.

| 1 | 2 | 3 | 4 | 5 |

28 I accept help if I think it would be beneficial (e.g. spiritual direction, counselling or help from friends).

| 1 | 2 | 3 | 4 | 5 |

29 I smile and laugh.

| 1 | 2 | 3 | 4 | 5 |

30 I feel content.

| 1 | 2 | 3 | 4 | 5 |

Cognitive and creative resilience (see chapter 8)

31 I am good at coming up with solutions to problems.

| 1 | 2 | 3 | 4 | 5 |

32 I am flexible when plans need to change.

| 1 | 2 | 3 | 4 | 5 |

33 I seek to continue learning (through experiences, study or reading the Bible and other books).

| 1 | 2 | 3 | 4 | 5 |

34 I have knowledge and expertise which I can draw on to help during difficult times.

| 1 | 2 | 3 | 4 | 5 |

35 I believe that good can come out of suffering.

| 1 | 2 | 3 | 4 | 5 |

36 I can reconcile suffering with my faith.

| 1 | 2 | 3 | 4 | 5 |

37 I am able to challenge unhelpful negative thoughts about myself or others.

| 1 | 2 | 3 | 4 | 5 |

38 I remind myself of uplifting biblical truths.

| 1 | 2 | 3 | 4 | 5 |

39 I am creative or imaginative (making up stories, carpentry, music, cooking, writing, gardening, art or crafts, etc.).

| 1 | 2 | 3 | 4 | 5 |

40 I seek God's wisdom, discernment or guidance.

| 1 | 2 | 3 | 4 | 5 |

Social and systemic resilience (see chapter 10)

41 I have at least one person I can confide in about anything.

1   2   3   4   5

42 My key relationships (e.g. with partner, friends, children, parents or siblings) are positive and supportive.

1   2   3   4   5

43 There are people who help me if I need help (practically or emotionally).

1   2   3   4   5

44 I do not feel socially isolated or lonely.

1   2   3   4   5

45 I am not anxious about security where I live.

1   2   3   4   5

46 I am not anxious about finance or work.

1   2   3   4   5

47 I am not anxious about government policies/actions.

1   2   3   4   5

48 I feel happy with my living conditions and I do not find the climate draining or difficult to cope with.

1   2   3   4   5

49 I believe that the culture I live in helps me to be resilient.

1   2   3   4   5

50 I am part of a helpful team, community or organisation that has good leadership.

1   2   3   4   5

Result

Total score for spiritual aspects (p. 172) _____

Total score for physical aspects (p. 173) _____

Total score for emotional aspects (p. 174) _____

Total score for cognitive and creative aspects (p. 175) _____

Total score for social and systemic aspects (p. 176) _____

OVERALL TOTAL _____

Look at your totals for the five domains. Which do you score most highly on, and which is your lowest score? Do you think this is an accurate portrayal of your strengths and weaknesses?

Look at the questions that you scored lowest on. Is there anything you can do to improve your resilience in these areas?

Looking at the entire questionnaire, choose two or three goals you can set yourself to improve your resilience.

Perhaps you could return to the questionnaire in six months to assess your progress.

Appendix B

Resilience creed

Many churches have a practice of reciting together the historic creeds of the church during their worship. In times of great difficulty, it is not so much these statements of faith that hold us firm but the things we believe in our hearts. Here are some truths from scripture that you may find helpful in strengthening your faith during times of hardship, suffering or adversity. You can change the pronoun from 'I' to 'We' if you wish to reflect the corporate nature of resilience. You may also say, 'I choose to believe' at the start of each declaration to show it is an act of faith. You may also add your own favourite scriptures.

I believe that God is working all things together for good.

I believe that nothing can separate me from the love of God that is mine in Christ Jesus.

I believe that I can do all things through Christ who gives me strength.

I believe that God is faithful, and will not let me be tempted beyond what I can bear, but will also provide a way of escape.

I believe that his grace is sufficient for me, and that his strength is made perfect in my weakness.

I believe that he who began a good work in me will bring it to completion.

I believe that nothing can take me from his hand.

I believe that Christ will never leave me nor forsake me.

I believe that in every circumstance the Holy Spirit is my comforter, counsellor and helper.

I believe that God will use trials to refine me and to make me stronger, wiser and more compassionate.

References
Romans 8:28; Romans 8:38-39; Philippians 4:13; 1 Corinthians 10:13; 2 Corinthians 12:9; Philippians 1:6; John 10:29; Hebrews 13:5; John 14:16; 1 Peter 1:6–7

Notes

1 Definition of resilience (UNICEF, 2011), cited in E. Fiddian-Qasmiyeh and A. Ager, *Local Faith Communities and the Promotion of Resilience in Humanitarian Situations: A scoping study*, Working paper series 90 (Oxford Refugee Studies Centre, 2013), p. 15.

2 M. Neenan and W. Dryden, 'What is resilience?' in M. Neenan, *Developing Resilience: A cognitive-behavioural approach* (Routledge, 2009), p. 17.

3 S. Timmins, *Developing Resilience in Young People with Autism using Social Stories* (Jessica Kingsley Publishers, 2017), p. 26.

4 E. Barrett and P. Martin, *Extreme: Why some people thrive at the limits* (Oxford University Press, 2014), p. 165.

5 K. Carr, 'Personal resilience', in F.C. Schaefer and C.A. Schaefer (eds), *Trauma and Resilience* (Condeo Press, 2012), p. 93.

6 D. Oates, 'What it takes to work abroad', *International Management*, 10 (1970), pp. 24–27 (p. 24).

7 First published in German in 1946: V. Frankl, *Man's Search for Meaning* (Random House, 2004).

8 M. Basoglu, S. Mineka, M. Paker, T. Aker, M. Livanou and S. Gök, 'Psychological preparedness for trauma as a protective factor in survivors of torture', *Psychological Medicine*, 27 (1997), pp. 1421–33.

9 K. Birkett, *Resilience: A spiritual project* (The Latimer Trust, 2016).

10 H. Nouwen, *The Inner Voice of Love* (Bantam Doubleday Dell, 1999), pp. 90–91.

11 See B.M. Gillespie, M. Chaboyer, M. Wallis and P. Grimbeek, 'Resilience in the operating room: developing and testing of a resilience model', *Journal of Advanced Nursing*, 59 (2007), pp. 427–38.

12 R.A. Bressan, E. Iacoponi, J. Candido de Assis and S.S. Shergill, 'Hope is a therapeutic tool', *British Medical Journal*, 359 (2017), p. j5469.

13 K. Sweeny, 'The downsides of positivity', *The Psychologist*, 30 (February 2017), pp. 30–35.

14 K. Carr, personal communication, 4 December 2017.

15 L. Bilinda, *The Colour of Darkness* (Hodder and Stoughton, 1996), pp. 97–8.

16 L. Bilinda, *With What Remains* (Hodder and Stoughton, 2006).

17 F. Luskin, *Forgive for Good: A proven prescription for health and happiness* (HarperCollins, 2002).

18 R.A. Emmons, *Thanks! How practicing gratitude can make you happier* (Houghton Mifflin Company, 2007).

19 Emmons, *Thanks!* p. 171.

20 T. Horsfall, *Working from a Place of Rest* (BRF, 2010).

21 M.J. Dawn, *Keeping the Sabbath Wholly* (Eerdmans Publishing, 1989).

22 R.A. Baer, 'Mindfulness training as a clinical intervention: a conceptual and empirical review', *Clinical Psychology: Science and practice*, 10 (2003), pp. 125–43; Barrett and Martin, *Extreme*, pp. 174–76; P.D. Larsen and D.C. Galletly, 'The sound of silence is music to the heart', *Heart*, 92 (2006), pp. 433–34.

23 L. Shanshan Li, M.J. Stampfer, D.R. Williams and T.J. Van der Weele, 'Association of religious service attendance with mortality among women', *JAMA Internal Medicine*, 176 (2016), pp. 777–85.

24 Fiddian-Qasmiych and Ager, *Local Faith Communities and the Promotion of Resilience in Humanitarian Situations*; T.B. Smith, M.E. McCullough and J. Poll, 'Religiousness and depression: Evidence for a main effect and the moderating influence of stressful life events'. *Psychological Bulletin*, 129 (2003), pp. 614–36.

25 See J.O. Hagberg and R.A. Guelich, *The Critical Journey: Stages in the life of faith* (Sheffield Publishing Company, 2005).

26 G. Thomas, *Sacred Pathways* (Thomas Nelson, 1982).

27 M. Perrine, *What's your God Language?* (Tyndale, 2007).

28 See R. Schnase, *Cultivating Fruitfulness* (Abingdon Press, 2008), pp. 43–58.

29 J. Clarke and J. Nicholson, *Resilience* (Crimson Publishing, 2010), p. 49.

30 Clarke and Nicholson, *Resilience*, p. 194.

31 J.I. Packer, *A Passion for Faithfulness* (Crossway, 2000), p. 93.

32 G. Wu, A. Feder, H. Cohen, J.J. Kim, S. Calderon, D.S. Charney and A.A. Mathé, 'Understanding resilience', *Frontiers in Behavioural Neuroscience*, 7 (2013), pp. 1–15.

33 P. Salmon, 'Effects of physical exercise on anxiety, depression, and sensitivity to stress: a unifying theory'. *Clinical Psychology Review*, 21 (2001), pp. 33–61.

34 NHS activity guidelines for adults at **nhs.uk/Livewell/fitness/Pages/**

physical-activity-guidelines-for-adults.aspx. Accessed 17 November 2017.

35   M. Nagai, S. Hoshide and K. Kario, 'Sleep duration as a risk factor for cardiovascular disease: a review of the recent literature', *Current Cardiology Reviews*, 6 (2010), pp. 54–61.

36   R. Leproult, G. Copinschi, O. Buxton and E. Van Cauter, 'Sleep loss results in an elevation of cortisol levels the next evening', *Sleep: Journal of sleep research and sleep medicine*, 20 (1997), pp.865–70.

37   Barrett and Martin, *Extreme*, pp. 47–49.

38   For more information see T.J. Sharp, *The Good Sleep Guide* (Penguin Books, 2001) and **nhs.uk/conditions/insomnia/self-help**. Accessed 23 November 2018.

39   See **gov.uk/rest-breaks-work**. Accessed 23 November 2017.

40   Barrett and Martin, *Extreme*, p. 181.

41   For information about healthy eating, see **nhs.uk/Livewell/ Goodfood/Pages/the-eatwell-guide.aspx**. Accessed 8 April 2018.

42   Department of Health, *UK Chief Medical Officers' Low Risk Drinking Guidelines*, 2016. Available at **gov.uk/government/uploads/system/ uploads/attachment_data/file/545937/UK_CMOs__report.pdf**. Accessed 15 November 2017.

43   NHS, *Water, Drinks and Your Health*, available at **nhs.uk/Livewell/ Goodfood/Pages/water-drinks.aspx**. Accessed 30 November 2017.

44   **talktofrank.com**. Accessed 13 April 2018.

45   T. Hartig, G.W. Evans, L.D. Jamner, D.S. Davis and T. Garling, 'Tracking restoration in natural and urban field settings', *Journal of Environmental Psychology*, 23 (2003), pp. 109–23.

46   R. Bragg and G. Atins, 'A review of nature-based interventions for mental health care', *Natural England Commissioned Reports*, 204 (2016).

47   M. Richardson, A. Cormack, L. McRobert and R. Underhill, '30 days wild: development and evaluation of a large-scale nature engagement campaign to improve well-being', *PLoS ONE*, 11 (18 February 2016), **doi.org/10.1371/journal.pone.0149777**. Accessed 16 January 2019.

48   R. Risner, *The Passing of the Night: My seven years as a prisoner of the North Vietnamese* (Ballantine Books, 2000), p. 183.

49   Barrett and Martin, *Extreme*, p. 169.

50   H.J. Polan and M.J. Ward, 'Role of the mother's touch in failure to thrive: a preliminary investigation', *Journal of the American Academy of Child and Adolescent Psychiatry*, 33 (1994), pp. 1098–105.

51   K.M. Grewen, B.J. Anderson, S.S. Girlder and K.C. Light, 'Warm partner contact is related to lower cardiovascular reactivity', *Behavioral Medicine*, 29 (2003), pp. 123–30.

52   D. Keltner, 'Hands on research: the science of touch', *Greater Good Magazine* (29 September 2010).

53   L. Artigas and I. Jarero, 'The butterfly hug method for bilateral stimulation', 2014. Available at **emdrresearchfoundation.org/ toolkit/butterfly-hug.pdf**. Accessed 16 January 2019.

54   J.W. Pennebaker, *Opening Up: The healing power of expressing emotions* (Guilford Press, 1997).

55   D.M. Hawker, J. Durkin and D.S.J. Hawker, 'To debrief or not to debrief our heroes: that is the question', *Clinical Psychology and Psychotherapy*, 18 (2010), pp. 453–63.

56   Deuteronomy 4:10–15. Some verses refer to Sinai as the mountain where the ten commandments were given. Sinai and Horeb are often considered to have been different names for the same place, or they may have referred to different sides of the same mountain.

57   A. Ehlers, R.A. Mayou, and B. Bryant, B, 'Psychological predictors of chronic posttraumatic stress disorder after motor vehicle accidents', *Journal of Abnormal Psychology*, 107 (1998), pp. 508–19; D.M. Lovell, 'Psychological adjustment among returned overseas aid workers', unpublished doctoral dissertation, 1997, University of Wales, Bangor.

58   K.J. Petrie, R.J. Booth, and J.W. Pennebaker, 'The immunological effects of thought suppression', *Journal of Personality and Social Psychology*, 75 (1998), pp. 1264–72.

59   Pennebaker, *Opening Up*; J.W. Pennebaker, J.K. Kiecolt-Glaser and R. Glaser, 'Disclosure of traumas and immune function: health implications for psychotherapy', *Journal of Consulting and Clinical Psychology*, 56 (1988), pp. 239–45. One meta-analysis has suggested that expressive writing has no effect, while other meta-analyses have found a positive effect. This may be due to differences in instructions given and participant factors, as discussed in Q. Lu and A.L. Stanton, 'How benefits of expressive writing vary as a function of writing instructions, ethnicity and ambivalence over emotional expression', *Psychology and Health*, 25 (2010), pp. 669–84.

60   J.W. Pennebaker and S.K. Beall, 'Confronting a traumatic event: toward an understanding of inhibition and disease', *Journal of Abnormal Psychology*, 95 (1986), pp. 274–81.

61   B.A. Esterling, M.H. Antoni, M.A. Fletcher, S. Margulies and N. Schneiderman, 'Emotional disclosure through writing or speaking

modulates latent Epstein-Barr virus antibodytiters', *Journal of Consulting and Clinical Psychology*, 62 (1994), pp. 130–40.

62 See A. Weems, *Psalms of Lament* (Westminster John Knox Press, 1999).

63 A. Wilson and R. Wilson, *The Life you Never Expected* (IVP, 2015), pp. 56–7.

64 C. ten Boom, *The Hiding Place* (Hodder and Stoughton, 1971), pp. 31–32.

65 T. Lutz, *Crying: The natural and cultural history of tears* (W.W. Norton and Co., 1999).

66 Information about slow breathing and a video demonstration are available at **anxietycoach.com/breathingexercise.html**. Accessed 5 December 2017.

67 M. Coxon, 'The problem with rumination', *The Psychologist*, 24 (2011), pp. 70–71; A. Newberg and M.R. Waldman, *Words Can Change Your Brain* (Plume, 2014).

68 See also 1 Thessalonians 5:11.

69 M.E.M. Haglund, P.S. Nestadt, N.S. Cooper, S.M. Southwick and D.S. Charney, 'Psychobiological mechanisms of resilience: relevance to prevention and treatment of stress-related psychopathology', *Development and Psychopathology*, 19 (2007), pp. 889–920 (p. 908).

70 'Transcript of Stephen Hawking's first Reith lecture', **news.bbc. co.uk/1/shared/bsp/hi/pdfs/25_01_16_hawking_reith_with_ shukmanv2.pdf**. Accessed 16 January 2019.

71 T.L. Kraft and S.D. Pressman, 'Grin and bear it: the influence of manipulated facial expression on the stress response', *Psychological Science*, 23 (2012), pp. 1372–78.

72 Barrett and Martin, *Extreme*.

73 S. Romundstad, S. Svebak, A. Holen and J. Holmen, 'A 15-year follow-up study of sense of humor and causes of mortality: the Nord-Trøndelag health study', *Psychosomatic Medicine*, 78 (2016), pp. 345–53.

74 L. Robinson, M. Smith and J. Segal, 'Laughter is the best medicine', Helpguide.org, 2017. Available at **helpguide.org/articles/mental-health/laughter-is-the-best-medicine.htm**. Accessed 5 December 2017; Barrett and Martin, *Extreme*, p. 173.

75 D.L. Nolte and R. Harris, *Children Learn What They Live* (Workman Publishing Company, 1998).

76 **fischy.com/songs-for-life/songs**. Accessed 16 January 2019.

77 Schaefer and Schaefer, *Trauma and Resilience*, pp. v-vi.

78 J. Allain-Chapman, *Resilient Pastors* (SPCK, 2012), p. 19.

79 Birkett, *Resilience*, p. 42.

80 B. Manning, *Ruthless Trust* (SPCK, 2002), pp. 3–4.

81 E. Peterson, *The Message of David* (Marshall Pickering, 1997), p. 105.

82 Birkett, *Resilience*, p.42.

83 P. Cuijpers, A. Van Straten and L. Warmerdam, 'Problem solving therapies for depression: a meta-analysis'. *European Psychiatry*, 22 (2007), pp. 9–15.

84 Z. Cooper, C.G. Fairburn and D.M. Hawker, *Cognitive-Behavioural Treatment of Obesity* (Guilford Press, 2003), p. 58.

85 For help with this, see J.P. Lederach, *The Little Book of Conflict Transformation* (Good Books, 2003).

86 See K. Sande, *The Peacemaker: A biblical guide to resolving personal conflict* (Baker Books, 1992).

87 C. Carr and J. James, *The Sky is Always There* (Canterbury Press, 2008); Personal conversation with Carr and James.

88 T. Waite, *Taken on Trust* (Hodder and Stoughton, 1993); Personal conversation with Waite.

89 See C.L. Park, M.A. Mills and D. Edmondson, 'PTSD as meaning violation: testing a cognitive worldview perspective'. *Psychological Trauma: Theory, research, practice, and policy*, 4 (2012), pp. 66–73.

90 D.A. Alexander and A. Wells, 'Reactions of police officers to body-handling after a major disaster: a before-and-after comparison', *British Journal of Psychiatry*, 159 (1991), pp. 547–55.

91 J. Eareckson Tada, 'Lessons from a hospital bed'. *Woman Alive* (August 2016), p. 30.

92 For example, J. Eareckson Tada, *A Step Further* (Pickering, 1984).

93 H. Roseveare, *Enough* (Christian Focus Publications, 2011), p. 27.

94 P. Greig, *God on Mute* (David Cook, 2007).

95 S.E. Shaum, *The Uninvited Companion* (Cresta Riposos Books, 2017).

96 T. Keller, *Walking with God through Pain and Suffering* (Hodder and Stoughton, 2013).

97 E.A. Holmes, E.L. James, T. Coode-Bate and C. Deeprose, 'Can playing the computer game "Tetris" reduce the build-up of flashbacks for trauma? A proposal from cognitive science'. PLoS One, 4 (2009), e4153; Personal communication with Holmes.

98 M. Lahad, M. Shacham and O. Ayalon (eds.), *The 'BASIC PH' Model of Coping and Resiliency* (Jessica Kingsley, 2012).

99 A. Frank, *The Diary of a Young Girl: Abridged for young readers* (Puffin, 2015), p. 242–43.

100 J.K. Rowling, *Very Good Lives* (Little, Brown and Co., 2015), p. 67.

101 S. Eenigenburg, *Screams in the Desert* (William Carey Library, 2007), p. 113.

102 Eenigenburg, *Screams in the Desert*, p. 114

103 See L. Carey, *Expressive and Creative Arts Methods for Trauma Survivors* (Jessica Kingsley, 2006).

104 See R. Parker, *Healing Dreams: Their power and purpose in your spiritual life* (SPCK, 2013).

105 C. Webster-Stratton, *Wally's Detective Book for Solving Problems at Home* (Seth, 1998); C. Webster-Stratton, *Wally's Detective Book for Solving Problems at School* (Seth, 1998).

106 S. Timmins, *Developing Resilience in Young People with Autism using Social Stories*.

107 **messychurch.org.uk**. For ideas to use at home, see **godventure. co.uk** and **faithinhomes.org.uk**. Accessed 14 April 2018.

108 J. Berryman, *Godly Play: An imaginative approach to religious education* (HarperSanFrancisco, 1991).

109 A. Begg, *The Hand of God* (Moody, 1999), p. 9.

110 E. Liddle, *Disciplines of the Christian Life* (SPCK, 2009), p. 122.

111 From the hymn 'O Love that will not let me go' by George Matheson (1842–1906).

112 S.E. Hobfoll, P. Watson, C.C. Bell et al., 'Five essential elements of immediate and mid-term mass trauma intervention: empirical evidence', *Psychiatry*, 70 (2007), pp. 283–315; C.R. Brewin, B. Andrews and J.D. Valentine, 'Meta analysis of risk factors for posttraumatic stress disorder in trauma exposed adults', *Journal of Consulting and Clinical Psychology*, 68 (2000), pp. 748–66; M.E.M. Haglund, P.S. Nestadt, N.S. Cooper, S.M. Southwick and D.S. Charney, 'Psychobiological mechanisms of resilience: Relevance to prevention and treatment of stress-related psychopathology'. *Development and Psychopathology*, 19 (2007), pp. 889–920.

113 Wilson and Wilson, *The Life You Never Expected*, p. 63.

114 N. Crawford and K. Carr, 'Understanding and enhancing the resilience of single mission personnel: learning from over 800 workers', in D. Hawker and T. Herbert (eds), *Single Mission: Thriving as a single person in cross-cultural ministry* (Condeo Press, 2013), pp. 233–41.

115 Crawford and Carr, 'Understanding and enhancing the resilience of single mission personnel', p. 234.

116 Crawford and Carr, 'Understanding and enhancing the resilience of

single mission personnel', pp. 234–35.

117 Crawford and Carr, 'Understanding and enhancing the resilience of single mission personnel', p. 236.

118 G. Thomas, *Sacred Marriage* (Zondervan, 2000).

119 K. O'Donnell (ed.), *Doing Member Care Well* (William Carey Library, 2002), p. 16.

120 D.M. Lovell, G. Hemmings and A.B. Hill, 'Bereavement reactions of female Scots and Swazis: a preliminary comparison', *British Journal of Medical Psychology*, 66 (1993), pp. 259–74.

121 R. Wilkinson and K. Pickett, 'How inequality hollows out the soul', *Clinical Psychology Forum*, 297 (September 2017), pp. 2–3.

122 Barrett and Martin, *Extreme*, pp. 115–16.

123 Barrett and Martin, *Extreme*, p. 22.

124 B. Avolio, F. Walumbwa and T. Weber, 'Leadership: current theories, research, and future directions'. *Annual Review of Psychology*, 60 (2009), pp. 421–49.

125 See B. Lewis, *Raising Children in a Digital Age* (Lion Books, 2014).

126 J. Lawrence, *Growing Leaders* (BRF, 2004).

127 **opendoorsuk.org**. Accessed 14 April 2018.

128 Schaefer and Schaefer, *Trauma and Resilience*, pp. 145–46.

129 W. Benn, *The Last Word* (Christian Focus, 1996), p. 30.

130 Peterson, *The Message of David*, p. 101.

131 Manning, *Ruthless Trust*, p. 6.

132 T. Tenney, *Hadassah: One night with the king* (BethanyHouse, 2004), p. 189.

133 R. Niebuhr, 'Serenity prayer', in *Narcotics Anonymous White Booklet* (Narcotics Anonymous, 1976).

134 P. Miller, *A Loving Life* (IVP, 2014), p. 24.

135 Miller, *A Loving Life*, p. 79.

136 BBC documentary, *The Coronation* with Coronation expert Alastair Bruce, shown on 31 January 2018.

137 S. Miller, 'Bald, blind and single?' *Christianity Today*, 47 (1995). Available at **christianitytoday.com/history/issues/issue-47**. Accessed 10 March 2018.

138 P. Hughes, *Commentary on Second Corinthians* (Eerdmans, 1962), p. 13.

139 P. Mallard, *Invest Your Suffering* (IVP, 2013), p. 82.

140 W. Nee, *The Collected Works of Watchman Nee, Set 3, Volume 56: The open door and the present testimony* (Living Stream Ministry, 1994), p. 449.

141 B. Manning, *Abba's Child* (NavPress, 1994), p. 61.

142 D. Runcorn, *Space for God* (Daybreak, 1990), p. 4.

143 T. Hewitt, *Commentary on Hebrews* (Tyndale Press, 1968), p. 191.

144 T. Herbert at **syzygy.org.uk/deep-roots**. Accessed 9 April 2018.

145 Barrett and Martin, *Extreme*, p. 166.

Servant Ministry
A portrait of Christ
and a pattern for his followers

Tony Horsfall

Servanthood is something to which all believers are called, not just those in full-time ministry. Understanding what servanthood means is thus vital for the health and well-being of local churches. Writing from many years of Christian teaching and mentoring, Tony Horsfall applies insights drawn from the first 'servant song' in Isaiah to topics such as the motivation for service and the call to serve; valid expressions of servanthood and the link between evangelism and social action; character formation and what it means to be a servant; how to keep going over the long haul in the harsh realities of ministry; and the importance of listening to God daily.

Servant Ministry
A portrait of Christ and a pattern for his followers
Tony Horsfall
978 0 85746 886 4 £8.99

brfonline.org.uk

A Fruitful Life

Abiding in Christ as seen in John 15

Tony Horsfall

Foreword by Steve Brady

A Fruitful Life ponders the teaching of Jesus in John 15, the famous 'vine' passage, as he prepares his disciples for his departure and describes how they can be effective witnesses in a hostile world. Just as Jesus' instructions revolutionised the lives of the first disciples, so a proper understanding of what he is saying can completely transform our lives also. It is the heart of the gospel message: the only way to live the Christian life is to allow Jesus to live his life in us and through us. This book includes material for individual reflection and questions for group discussion.

A Fruitful Life
Abiding in Christ as seen in John 15
Tony Horsfall
978 0 85746 884 0 £8.99

brfonline.org.uk

Transforming
lives and communities

Christian growth and understanding of the Bible

Resourcing individuals, groups and leaders in churches for their own spiritual journey and for their ministry

Church outreach in the local community

Offering two programmes that churches are embracing to great effect as they seek to engage with their local communities and transform lives

Teaching Christianity in primary schools

Working with children and teachers to explore Christianity creatively and confidently

Children's and family ministry

Working with churches and families to explore Christianity creatively and bring the Bible alive **parenting for faith**

Visit **brf.org.uk** for more information on BRF's work

brf.org.uk